'There is no such thing as a "self-made man/woman". We are made up of thousands of others. Everyone who has ever done a kind deed for us, or spoken one word of encouragement to us, has entered into the make-up of our character and of our thoughts, as well as our success.'

– unknown

Thank you for all of the support
and love along the way. This is
for every single one of you. xx

HAPPY FOOD

FAST, FRESH, SIMPLE VEGAN

BETTINA CAMPOLUCCI BORDI

PHOTOGRAPHY BY NASSIMA ROTHACKER

hardie grant books

CONTENTS

MY STORY

My earliest memories are of growing up in East Africa (Tanzania). Barely wearing shoes, spending weekends on the beach, following my mother to the local markets in the pursuit of the freshest, best-quality fruits and vegetables, and haggling with the stallholders to get the best possible price. My mother was sharp and pretty hardcore when it came to negotiating, and everyone at the markets always knew she was coming.

Looking back at it now I can appreciate how lucky I was and what an idyllic childhood I was able to experience. Food was a big part of family life; my parents were good cooks. Growing up in a multi-cultural home – with a Norwegian father and a Danish/Bulgarian mother – I experienced an array of different food traditions. Our trips to see family, and our holidays in general, always revolved around what we ate, which restaurants we visited and what exciting new flavours we experienced. My Norwegian grandmother – who lived in Sweden – would forage and pick what she had available in her garden and knock up home-made jams, cordials and pickles, while my Bulgarian grandmother would cook up a feast for every major national holiday, choosing the freshest produce she could get hold of in the local market.

For me, I think cooking really began when I was six years old and had mastered the art of cooking pancakes, which I would proudly demo at breakfast to all my friends who came over for sleepovers. I was gifted a children's cookbook and that was it – I was hooked. Then at the tender age of 11 my family relocated to Sweden, and this began an escape into the kitchen. I vividly remember this period of my life, which I'd describe as taking a palm tree and placing it at the North Pole. The differences between Africa and Scandinavia were not only visible but could be felt by my little heart.

The change was enormous, and for the first six months I disliked my new life. I found it very difficult to adjust. First of all my background was a mish-mash; I had olive-coloured skin and my hair was much darker than that of the Swedish kids. I also had pretty distinct features, such as prominent eyes and nose. I experienced first hand what 'being different' felt like, and it took a while to get used to. My grandmother stayed with us a lot during this period, and I would seek solace in helping her cook, experimenting with using the fruits of the three apple trees in our garden.

Throughout my school years, cooking was the one skill I knew I was good at and could always trust. During my teens, my parents created a competition where each of us had to cook on alternate weekends. We were each given a budget and within it we had to create a three-course dinner in a set amount of time. This was when I really learnt how to follow recipes and my passion for cooking was awakened. Then, later, I cooked at my parents' dinner parties, in the communal kitchens at university, and I catered for my friends' birthday celebrations.

I was always on the lookout for foodie experiences, so I started working in the food and beverage industry, which transitioned me to study Hotel Management – I had discovered a study course that combined theory with the practicality I loved.

At 23, during my last year at university in Spain, I met my husband, who is half Italian and half English and shares my passion for food, coming from a family that has owned restaurants for generations. I decided to stay in the country after I finished my studies, working in different industries for a few years until I started my first little business, called Pockets. Through this

I catered to the ever-growing property offices on the Spanish coast, delivering home-made sandwiches and salads. In the summers I catered for the yachts and had another little business called Yacht Hampers. Both went well until the recession hit and many of the offices closed down. This period is now a blur; I tried to find work wherever I could but I didn't really know what I wanted to do in my life. I knew I had the potential to do something that would bring meaning to my soul, I just didn't know how to get there.

So I started working in event management, working crazy hours and running several projects at once. As many of you probably know, this is a tiring industry and at 26 I suffered a string of health issues. A visit to a gynaecologist confirmed that I suffered from polycystic ovary syndrome and endometriosis. I was told that the likelihood of me ever getting pregnant would be next to none and that this was a fate I should prepare myself for. Shocked, to say the least, I knew something had to change. It was also during this time that an opportunity to run health retreats arose. So I quit and embarked on co-founding and running those.

Because of my fondness and passion for food and cooking I was responsible to cook at these retreats. The guidelines were simple: the food had to be 100 per cent plant-based, meaning no animal products whatsoever, gluten-free and free from white sugar. Loving a challenge, I dug into cookbooks and blogs and started finding solutions to these issues, but because I was dealing with my own health condition, I found I was uncovering ways to deal with my symptoms in a natural way, too.

Seven months into the new venture and against all odds, I got pregnant. I am not into labels and would not call myself a vegan, but most of what I eat on a daily basis consists of plant-based foods, and while I don't want to make any claims that these foods helped me to get pregnant, what I can say for sure is that since adding more fruits, vegetables and general plant-based foods into my diet, I feel heaps better. I also cut out gluten around this time, after learning that I had probably been intolerant to it for a very long time, and this was what had been causing the stomach problems I had suffered from for as long as I can remember.

I continued to co-run and cook at health retreats for another three years until a good friend of mine, and later my business partner, Mark, encouraged me to pursue my passion. I listened then decided to blindly follow my heart, and thus Bettina's Kitchen was born. I developed my skills on the job by doing courses with the Matthew Kenney Culinary institute, based in Los Angeles, and also started documenting my recipes on social media so that I would remember them. Through this medium I shared my knowledge and created workshops to teach the basics of plant-based foods and how to incorporate them into your everyday life. Along the way I also encountered numerous clients who suffered intolerances and simply did not know how to replace what they had always had as a part of their diet – such as milk, flour and eggs.

In the last few years I have worked as a recipe consultant, written articles about how to incorporate plants into your everyday life, conducted pop-up workshops and freelanced and run several health retreats in numerous countries. My passion and expertise lies in how to use everyday ingredients and make them tasty in the simplest possible way. I love finding solutions and ways of cooking ingredients that I would normally never think of, as well as sourcing and finding seasonal fruits and vegetables and creating something yummy!

Cooking at retreats that are sometimes in remote places with limited access to equipment has taught me to make the most out of my ingredients and to not overcomplicate food. I want everyone to have a chance to cook from scratch with ingredients that can be found in any supermarket. I am passionate about ingredients; their source, their tastes and functionality and how to make them appeal to all tastes. When I was younger I desperately wanted to become an artist. I guess I found a way to express what my heart feels on every plate that comes out of my kitchen.

This book is a piece of my passion that I hope you will love as much as I do.

Lots of love,

Bettina

WHAT IS HAPPY FOOD?

Happy Food is a cookbook for everyone! Grandmothers with newly-converted vegan granddaughters coming over for Sunday dinner, couples who want to increase their veggie intake, single people looking for a quick meal after a long day, families that have allergens but want to enjoy a meal together without compromises on comfort and taste, as well as anyone who wants to give vegan or gluten-free cooking a go.

I have developed and cooked all the recipes in this book over the last six years, having cooked them for clients and family members, at pop-ups, workshops and more! The ingredients are few and all the methods are short, easy and quick.

These dishes are a combination of my philosophies. You feast with your eyes first, so making food look pretty on your plate is important when it comes to self-care and it is a lovely touch when cooking for yourself, family or friends. When it comes to flavour, I try as much as possible to combine the five tastes – sweet, sour, salty, spicy and bitter – in order to satisfy the tastebuds and offer the ultimate foodie experience. Texture is also super important – a bit of crunch on a curry, a dollop of creaminess on porridge and a drizzle of syrup on pancakes create an extra layer in a dish that makes it more fun and interesting.

Most of all, though, I believe that food is meant to make you happy! Whether it's love at first sight because it's so pretty or colourful, or at the first hit of flavour when the food bursts in your mouth, food is here to put a smile on our faces. Ingredients make me excited and happy and I hope that this eclectic collection will put a smile on your faces, too.

HOW TO USE THIS BOOK

Favourite Basics
This chapter is for all of you who would like to create everything from scratch. These really useful recipes can be prepared ahead and stored for a long period in the pantry, fridge or even freezer – and you can use these wherever they are referred to in the ingredients' lists of other recipes throughout the book. If you prefer to use shop-bought products, such as gluten-free flour mix or plant yoghurts or milks, that would work, too. If you are not vegan or gluten-free and want to replace the dairy foods with animal products, that is absolutely fine, but I would recommend that you always buy good-quality products – preferably organic. In terms of my baked goods, if you are not using gluten-free flour mixes I would advise to use old, traditional grains such as spelt, Kamut and einkorn for best results. Give these basics a go, they are brilliant!

Waste not
Many of the recipes in this book – specifically the Home Alone chapter (page 42) – are dedicated to serving smaller amounts. Families of two or fewer have been accounted for, so as to not waste ingredients and so that you don't have to eat the same meal over a few days as leftovers! I have also tried to make use of a smaller selection of ingredients throughout the book, so that if you buy 500 g (1 lb 2 oz) of carrots you are not limited to using them in only one recipe. I have on several occasions hunted down certain condiments, salts or spices for one particular dish and ended up not using them again, which over time creates a

great pantry with an eclectic collection of weird and wonderful ingredients, but one where many of the contents go to waste!

Short cuts

I do not expect any of you to be domestic goddesses and spend hours upon hours in the kitchen unnecessarily, so it's ok to buy pre-cooked pulses and grains if that will save you time and fuss. Just make sure you choose good-quality ones.

I have specified certain ingredients in the book, but there is a reason for it, I promise! For example, buying coconut milk in a Tetra Pak will be different to buying it in a tin. Medjool dates versus 'normal dates' also makes a huge difference in taste and texture.

TIPS AND TRICKS

Buy in bulk

As work has got busier, the time I set aside to go shopping for ingredients has become limited. Therefore I started buying certain products that have a long shelf-life in bulk, such as nuts, seeds, grains and pulses. Not only does it save me time but it is also easier on my wallet. This has been made even simpler with the option of ordering ingredients online and getting stuff delivered to your door.

Get the best ingredients you can buy

I always try to source organic and seasonal produce, no matter where in the world I am and regardless of whether it's for my own consumption or for work. I do this for a number of reasons. First of all, I love to see where my produce has been grown and all the hard work that went into it. Secondly, I love supporting local and small producers that grow seasonal vegetables. Last but not least, you can taste the difference! Nonetheless, I do understand that not everyone is as passionate as I am, or perhaps doesn't have the time to go out and source such suppliers. Eating organic in a city can be expensive, too, as unfortunately it comes with a certain price tag.

So here are some quick tips to make sure you are buying the best you can afford:

Find a local farm that delivers seasonal fruit and veggie boxes to your door.

Don't go 100 per cent organic, but buy what you can afford and make sure the rest is as fresh and good-quality as it can be.

Find out what's in season, often those foods will be well priced.

Choose quality over quantity – it makes a difference!

Do all of your shopping for the week in one go. Farmers' markets have become pretty popular over the last few years. Find one and stock up for your week of cooking. (PS: If you are there at the end of the day, when the stallholders are packing up, most fresh food vendors want to get rid of their produce and will offer you a good deal!)

One thing I have noticed is that organic produce lasts a lot longer in your fridge compared to the pre-packed stuff. That's not a claim, just an observation from years of experience.

PREPARATION

Preparation is key. Having some of the basic recipes in the book already prepped and stored will cut the time spent cooking on another day. Try to do one big fruit and veg shop that will last you all week, and make sure your pantry is well stocked with the good-quality basic ingredients all the time. (See opposite for my pantry basics.)

EQUIPMENT

You won't need fancy equipment to begin with, as these recipes simply don't demand it. When I first started cooking as a freelance chef I had hand-held blender and that was it! It helps if you have a good blender, especially when making the cheeses, yoghurts and some of the dressings, but they can be also be made using regular blenders – it will just take an extra blitz or two. Otherwise, all you need is a kitchen, bowls, pots and pans and you're good to go!

PANTRY BASICS

Here is a list of basics that I keep stocked in my cupboards at all times, as they are all good long-life ingredients. Don't go buying them all in one go; I suggest you start off slowly with the ones you know that you love and will use, then add to these as you become more confident in the kitchen and adopt new tastes.

Seeds
Chia
Flaxseed – golden/brown
Hemp hearts
Pumpkin
Sesame – white or black
Sunflower

Nuts
Almonds
Brazils
Cacao nibs
Cashews
Hazelnuts
Macadamias
Peanuts
Pecans
Pistachios
Walnuts

Grains & pulses
Black beans (tinned or dried)
Buckwheat
Butter beans (lima beans)
   (tinned or dried)
Chickpeas (garbanzo beans
   (tinned or dried)
Millet
Oats
Quinoa
Red lentils (tinned or dried)
Rice – black, white and brown

Oils
Coconut oil
Grapeseed oil
Olive oil – the greener the better

Flours
Almond flour & meal
Brown rice flour
Buckwheat flour
Chickpea flour (gram flour)
Oat flour
Potato flour & starch
Tapioca flour
White rice flour

Milks
There are lots to choose from, so pick your favourite. My preferred milks are:
Almond
Coconut (buy this in Tetra Pak, it
   makes a difference)

Spices & baking ingredients
100% cacao powder
Baking powder
Bicarbonate of soda
   (baking soda)
Black peppercorns
Cardamom (ground and seeds)
Chilli flakes (red pepper flakes)
Cinnamon (ground and sticks)
Cloves (whole)
Nutmeg (the whole nut
   rather than the powder)
Rose water
Sea salt (the real deal)
   and Himalayan sea salt
Sumac
Sweet paprika
Turmeric

Vanilla pod (bean)/paste/powder
   (not the sweet white powder
   but the proper dried vanilla
   pod powder)

Sweeteners
Dates (use medjool whenever
   possible – it makes a
   huge difference)
Maple syrup
Stevia (for diabetics)
Yacun syrup (an option
   for diabetics)

Condiments
Dijon mustard
Nutritional yeast (totally optional
   and known as vegan crack, this
   makes everything taste a bit
   better and cheesier)
Tamari (gluten-free soy sauce)

Other dry goods
Good-quality gluten-free pasta
   (the yellower the better, I find)
Rice noodles

Fresh herbs
Try to buy living pots of these for
a windowsill, or in the garden:
Basil
Dill
Mint
Parsley
Rocket (arugula)
Rosemary
Thyme

HAPPY

START

HAPPY START

Breakfast is my favourite meal of the day. The morning is a time to recuperate after a long night's sleep, to nourish your body and give it what it needs to cope with what lies in store for the rest of the day. It's also when we're at our busiest; rushing around getting ready. So that's why efficiency and ease are the way to go. In this chapter there are a variety of my best-loved recipes that are both savoury and sweet, hot and cold, easy and quick. Some can be pre-prepared or even batch-cooked and frozen to get ahead without compromising on taste. I have also added some shortcuts so that you can make use of all the ingredients you buy without any waste!

BATCH COOKABLE

FREEZABLE

LASTS FOR +3 DAYS
IN THE FRIDGE

CAN BE NUT-FREE IF
YOU USE COCONUT
MILK INSTEAD OF
ALMOND

BRIGHT HEALING TURMERIC PORRIDGE & WARM BERRIES

This recipe is a great way of including turmeric in your diet. This funky combination incorporates centuries-old Ayurvedic healing knowledge combined with a new twist on an old classic. Give it a try – if, like me, you love the taste of the Orient, this will be right up your street.

Serves 2

110 g (4 oz / ½ cup) millet
250 ml (8 fl oz / 1 cup) water
160 ml (5 fl oz / ⅔ cup) Almond
  Milk or any plant milk, shop-
  bought or home-made
  (see pages 137–139)
1 teaspoon ground turmeric
pinch of black pepper
1 teaspoon coconut oil, melted

For the warm berries
100 g (3½ oz) each raspberries
  and blueberries
1 tablespoon maple syrup
½ vanilla pod (bean), scraped,
  or ½ teaspoon ground vanilla pod

To serve
a dollop of Coconut Yoghurt,
  shop-bought or home-made
  (see page 142)
chopped nuts (hazelnuts
  or pistachios)
micro herbs and edible flowers
  (optional)

Place the millet and the water in a saucepan over high heat and bring to the boil. Let it simmer for 5 minutes until the millet thickens and there is almost no water left.

Add the milk, turmeric, pepper and melted coconut oil and bring to the boil. As soon as the mixture starts to boil, leave the porridge to bubble away until you get a beautiful, creamy, golden porridge.

Warm berries While the porridge is simmering, put the berries, maple syrup and pinch of vanilla seeds or powder into a small saucepan and gently heat. Cook until the berries begin to soften, then mash some of the berries until you get a lovely sauce, leaving a few berries whole.

Ladle the porridge into the bowls, add a helping of warm berries, a dollop of coconut yoghurt and sprinkle with chopped nuts – my favourite for this porridge is pistachios but any will do – and some micro herbs and edible flowers, if using.

Tip This recipe can easily be made in a larger quantity and reheated with a splash of plant milk (see pages 137–139 for home-made nut milks).

BATCH COOKABLE

FREEZABLE

LASTS FOR +3 DAYS
IN THE FRIDGE

SLOW-COOKED OATS & BUCKWHEAT PORRIDGE WITH CARAMELISED APPLE

I love a good porridge on a cold winter's morning. I also love savoury breakfasts with a dash of sweetness. This porridge is equivalent to a warm embrace and makes the best start on a rainy day.

Serves 2

140 g (5 oz / ⅔ cup) milled
   gluten-free oats
80 g (3 oz / ⅓ cup) whole
   buckwheat
½ vanilla pod (bean), scraped,
   or ½ teaspoon ground vanilla pod
pinch of salt

For the quick almond milk
60 g (2½ oz / ⅓ cup) almonds
500 ml (18 fl oz / 2 cups) water
pinch of ground cardamom
pinch of grated nutmeg

For the caramelised apple topping
1 apple, peeled, cored and diced
1 tablespoon coconut oil
2 tablespoons maple syrup
½ teaspoon ground cinnamon

To serve (optional)
dollop of Coconut Yoghurt,
   shop-bought or home-made
   (see page 142)
toasted chopped nuts and seeds

Almond milk   First make the almond milk. Place the almonds, water, cardamom and nutmeg in a blender and blitz until you get a frothy milk.

Put the oats, buckwheat, vanilla and pinch of salt in a saucepan and pour over the milk, pulp and all. Pop the pan on a medium heat and slowly bring to the boil, then lower the heat and simmer for 5–10 minutes.

Caramelised apple   While the porridge is simmering, add the diced apple to a hot pan with the coconut oil and start lightly browning. Once they are semi-soft, drizzle over the maple syrup and sprinkle over the cinnamon, then set aside.

Once the porridge has a creamy texture, ladle into bowls and top with the caramelised apple and optional add-ins, such as coconut yoghurt and toasted nuts and seeds.

BATCH COOKABLE

FREEZABLE

3–4 DAYS

LASTS FOR 3–4 DAYS
IN THE FRIDGE

PEANUT BUTTER OVERNIGHT OATS & HOME-MADE GRANOLA CRUNCH

I love a good porridge but in summertime when the weather gets a bit warmer, overnight oats are the perfect cool alternative.

Serves 2

1 tablespoon peanut butter
250 ml (8½ fl oz / 2⅓ cup) water
220 g (8 oz / 1 cup) gluten-free milled oats
1 medjool date, stoned (pitted) and chopped
1 tablespoon chopped toasted hazelnuts
½ vanilla pod (bean), scraped, or ½ teaspoon ground vanilla pod

For the granola crunch (makes a batch for a 450 g / 1 lb jar)
1 ripe banana, mashed
60 ml (2 fl oz / ¼ cup) melted coconut oil
60 ml 2 fl oz / ¼ cup) maple syrup
½ teaspoon ground cinnamon
120 g (4 oz / 1¼ cup) gluten-free milled oats
20 g (¾ oz / ¼ cup) desiccated (shredded) coconut
60 g (2 oz / ½ cup) chopped walnuts
60 g (2 oz / ¼ cup) whole buckwheat
40 g (1½ oz / ¼ cup) black sesame seeds
½ tablespoon grated orange zest

To serve
fruits and berries
chopped nuts and seeds
edible flowers (optional)

Mix the peanut butter with the water in a bowl. Then add the rest of the overnight oat ingredients, give it a mix and cover. Place in the fridge overnight.

Granola crunch
Now make the granola crunch. Preheat the oven to 140°C (275°F/Gas 1).

In a bowl, stir together the mashed banana, melted coconut oil, maple syrup and cinnamon. Make sure you have an even mixture without any lumps.

Add all the dry ingredients to the mixture except the sesame seeds and orange zest. Make sure everything is well incorporated with the banana mix.

Line a large baking tray (baking sheet) with greaseproof paper (wax paper). Tip the crunch mixture onto the tray, spreading it out evenly, and bake for 40 minutes. Check it every 10 minutes to make sure it's not getting burnt. Once the mixture is dry and crispy, it's done.

Remove from the oven and leave to cool on the tray. Once cool, stir in the orange zest and sesame seeds. Transfer to a large glass jar with an airtight lid. Alternatively, store it in a ziplock bag in the freezer, which will keep it fresh and crispy for longer.

Serve the overnight oats with a handful of granola crunch and choose from any of the serving options. I always tend to go slightly over the top with extra nut butter, berries, nuts, seeds and edible flowers.

Tip
This breakfast can be made in a bigger batch and lasts for 3–4 days in the fridge. It's a perfect takeaway breakfast or snack.

BATCH COOKABLE

FREEZABLE

+3 DAYS

LASTS FOR +3 DAYS IN THE FRIDGE

CAN BE NUT-FREE IF YOU USE COCONUT MILK INSTEAD OF ALMOND

HEARTY BUCKWHEAT WAFFLES WITH STRAWBERRIES

I love this breakfast, especially on a lazy weekend morning. It ticks all my boxes in terms of comfort, indulgence and appeasing that insatiable sweet tooth that we all have.

Makes 4 waffles, serves 2

60 ml (2 fl oz / ¼ cup) melted coconut oil, plus 1 tablespoon for the waffle iron
375 ml (13 fl oz / 1½ cups) Almond Milk, shop-bought or home-made (see page 139)
200 g (7 oz / 1⅓ cups) buckwheat flour
3 tablespoons cacao powder
½ teaspoon baking powder
½ vanilla pod (bean), scraped, or ½ teaspoon ground vanilla pod
pinch of salt

To serve
230 g (8 oz / 1 cup) Coconut Yoghurt, shop-bought or home-made (see page 142)
1 teaspoon grated lemon zest
1 tablespoon maple syrup, plus extra for drizzling
½ vanilla pod (bean), scraped, or ½ teaspoon ground vanilla pod
handful of fresh fruit
micro herbs and edible flowers (optional)

Start by heating the coconut oil in a pan on medium heat with the almond milk.

Place all the remaining waffle ingredients, including the melted coconut oil and almond milk, into a bowl and mix well.

Heat up the waffle iron and dab or brush with coconut oil. I use the small waffle iron where the waffles come out looking like a four-leaf clover. Ladle some of the batter mixture into the iron and cook until super crispy.

While the waffles are cooking, pimp up the coconut yoghurt with lemon zest, maple syrup and the vanilla, stirring to combine.

Once the waffles have been cooked, serve with a dollop of the coconut yoghurt, fruits, micro herbs and edible flowers, if using, and drizzle with maple syrup.

BATCH COOKABLE

FREEZABLE

+3 DAYS

LASTS FOR +3 DAYS
IN THE FRIDGE

PANCAKES CAN BE
NUT-FREE IF YOU
USE COCONUT
MILK INSTEAD OF
ALMOND IN THE
BATTER

BANANA PANCAKES WITH HOME-MADE NUT-ELLA

One of my all-time favourite breakfasts. The grated apple adds sweetness to the batter and the caramelised bananas make these pancakes irresistible. Perfect for a lazy weekend morning, or you can batch-cook them and keep them, covered, in the fridge so you have breakfast sorted for a few days.

Makes 6 small pancakes, serves 2

140 g (5 oz / generous 1 cup)
 Gluten-free Flour Mix
 (see page 146)
250 ml (8 fl oz / 1 cup) Almond
 Milk or any plant milk,
 shop-bought or home-made
 (see pages 137–139)
½ teaspoon baking powder
pinch of salt
½ grated apple
½ vanilla pod (bean), scraped,
 or ½ teaspoon ground vanilla pod
1 tablespoon coconut oil, for frying
1–2 ripe bananas, sliced into rounds

For the nut-ella
 (makes a 700 g / 1 lb 9 oz jar)
300 g (10½ oz / 2 cups) hazelnuts
250 ml (8 fl oz / 1 cup) coconut oil
3–4 tablespoons maple syrup
3 tablespoons cacao powder
½ vanilla pod (bean), scraped,
 or ½ teaspoon ground vanilla pod

To serve
fresh fruit and berries
Coconut Yoghurt, shop-bought or
 home-made (see page 142)
drizzle of maple syrup
nuts and seeds
fresh mint leaves

Nut-ella Start with the nut-ella. Place the hazelnuts in a blender and blitz until fine. Then add the rest of the ingredients and blend to a smooth chocolate paste. Spoon into a clean glass jar or container and set aside.

Banana pancakes Add all the pancake ingredients, except the coconut oil and bananas, to a bowl and mix until you get a lovely thick pancake batter.

Using a pastry brush or kitchen paper (paper towel), rub a non-stick frying pan (skillet) with an even layer of coconut oil and pop on medium heat. Ladle in enough batter to make three small pancakes, arrange some banana slices on top and gently push them into the batter.

Cook the pancakes for 4–5 minutes until the batter sets, then gently flip the pancakes and cook for another 4–5 minutes until the bananas have caramelised and the pancakes are cooked through. Remove and keep warm. Repeat with the remaining batter and bananas until both are used up.

Serve the pancakes warm with a dollop of home-made nut-ella, fresh fruits and mint leaves. I also love adding a dollop of coconut yoghurt, a cheeky drizzle of maple syrup and some nuts or seeds.

BATCH COOKABLE

+3
DAYS

LASTS FOR +3 DAYS
IN THE FRIDGE

ALMOND BUTTER
& SMASHED RASPBERRY
STUFFED FRENCH TOAST

French toast was always a very comforting
breakfast when I was growing up. Here is
a version that includes a spark of freshness
from the berries along with some indulgence
and creaminess from the nut butter.

Serves 2

4 slices of Super Bread
  (see page 148) or good quality,
  shop-bought bread
160 ml (5 fl oz / ⅔ cup) almond or
  plant milk
1 tablespoon maple syrup,
  plus more for drizzling
1 tablespoon buckwheat flour
1 teaspoon ground cinnamon
¼ teaspoon freshly ground nutmeg
tiny pinch of salt
coconut oil, for frying

For the filling
4 tablespoons Almond Butter,
  shop-bought or home-made
  (see page 141)
1 punnet of raspberries

To serve
coconut sugar
dollop of Coconut Yoghurt,
  shop-bought or home-made
  (see page 142)
chopped nuts

First spread all 4 slices of bread with almond butter and squash as many raspberries as you can
fit in over 2 pieces of bread, then press them down with a fork. Top with the other slices and
gently press down.

In a small bowl, whisk together the almond milk, maple syrup, flour, cinnamon, nutmeg and
pinch of salt. Place the bread in a shallow dish (with sides) that holds all of the bread. Pour the
batter over the bread, then lift or flip it over to make sure both sides are evenly coated.

Heat a drizzle of coconut oil in a large frying pan (skillet) over medium heat. When the pan is
hot, add the bread slices and cook for a few minutes each side until golden brown.

To make it look pretty, cut your toast in half and serve scattered with coconut sugar and fruit
and drizzled with maple syrup and a dollop of coconut yoghurt and some chopped nuts, or just
have it as it is.

PISTACHIO MILK CHIA PUDDING IN A JAR

Chia puddings are a great quick breakfast, especially for those suffering from porridge fatigue. This is a quick version with a twist – add whatever toppings or milk you like. Pistachio is one of my favourite milks but it isn't one that you can buy in shops, which makes this twist extra special.

Serves 2

60 g (2 oz / ⅓ cup) raw shelled
  pistachio nuts
250 ml (8 fl oz / 1 cup) water
½ vanilla pod (bean), scraped,
  or ½ teaspoon ground vanilla pod
1 teaspoon maple syrup
a dash of rose water (optional)
5 tablespoons chia seeds

To serve
Granola Crunch (see page 22)
nut butter, shop-bought or
  home-made (see page 141)
berries or cherries

Place the pistachios, water, vanilla seeds or powder, maple syrup and rose water (if using) in a blender and blitz until you have a light green milk.

Put the chia seeds in a jar and cover with the pistachio milk, pulp and all. Pop the lid on and give it a good shake.

You can leave the jar in the fridge overnight or wait for at least 30 minutes until the chia seeds absorb all the liquid and you are left with a lovely thick consistency.

Top off your jar with any of the serving alternatives. My personal favourites are granola crunch, a dollop of nut butter and berries or slices of orange.

Tip

This is a fantastic takeaway breakfast, perfect for eating on the go. It can be made in bigger batches and lasts in the fridge for at least 3–4 days, giving you breakfast for most of the week. Alternate your toppings and milks to find your favourite combination. Also, chia seeds are great bought in bulk.

BATCH COOKABLE

FREEZABLE

LASTS FOR +5 DAYS
IN THE FRIDGE

ONE-CUP STICKY BANANA BREAD

Guilty of being a banana bread lover?
I wanted to create a lighter version of the
classic. I think (if I may say so myself) that
this version rocks. I hope you love it as
much as I do.

Cuts into 8 slices

2 carrots, peeled and sliced
200 g (7 oz / 2 cups) almond flour
140 g (5 oz / 1 cup) Gluten-free
  Flour Mix (see page 146)
250 ml (8 fl oz / 1 cup) Almond Milk
  or any plant milk, shop-bought or
  home-made (see pages 137–139)
200 g (7 oz / 1 cup) coconut sugar
125 ml (4 fl oz / ½ cup) melted
  coconut oil
1 teaspoon ground cinnamon
½ teaspoon baking powder
½ teaspoon bicarbonate of soda
  (baking soda)
½ teaspoon ground cloves
1 teaspoon ground cardamom
1 teaspoon vanilla pod (bean),
  scraped, or ground vanilla
pinch of salt

For the topping
1 banana, thinly sliced
  horizontally into 3
pinch of coconut sugar
1 ground vanilla pod (bean)

To serve
Almond Butter, shop-bought
  or home-made (see page 141)
dollop of Coconut Yoghurt,
  shop-bought or home-made
  (see page 142)
your favourite fruits

Preheat the oven to 180°C (350°F/Gas 4). Grease and line a 900 g (2 lb) loaf tin,
or use a silicone mould.

Start by boiling the carrots, then once soft, purée in a food processor and measure out
125 g (4 oz / ½ cup) and set aside.

Add all the other bread ingredients to a food processor, including the puréed carrots and
blitz together until you have a lovely smooth mixture.

Pour the mixture into the loaf tin, and place the banana slices carefully on top. Sprinkle over
the coconut sugar and ground vanilla.

Bake for 40–45 minutes. When ready it should feel firm and a toothpick inserted into the
centre of the cake should come out clean. Once out of the oven, let the cake cool a little,
then turn it out of the tin and let it cool completely on a wire rack.

Enjoy as it is or with any of the serving alternatives, such as nut butter, a dollop of coconut
yoghurt or some fruit.

Keep the cake in a covered airtight container in the fridge. Not that it will last you long!

BATCH COOKABLE

FREEZABLE

+3
DAYS

LASTS FOR +3 DAYS
IN THE FRIDGE

CHICKPEA OMELETTE, ROCKET, AVOCADO & MANGO SALSA

Doubt no more, this is the perfect weekend brunch dish. Excellent as a savoury breakfast when you're craving a filling meal. Having lots of clients suffering with allergies, this was the best egg swap I could come up with.

Makes 1 big omelette, serves 1

70 g (2½ oz / ½ cup) chickpea (gram) flour
125 ml (4 fl oz / ½ cup) water
½ teaspoon salt
a small pinch of ground turmeric (for colour)
½ tablespoon apple cider vinegar
½ teaspoon bicarbonate of soda (baking soda)
1 shallot, finely chopped
¼ red (bell) pepper, finely chopped
olive oil, for frying

For the filling
handful of rocket (arugula) or baby spinach
1 avocado, sliced
1 small spring onion (scallion), chopped
1 tablespoon pomegranate seeds, optional

For the mango salsa
1 tomato, finely chopped
½ mango, flesh finely chopped
1 tablespoon chopped coriander (cilantro)
salt and black pepper, to taste
½ red chilli, chopped
drizzle of olive oil

Start by putting all the omelette ingredients into a bowl except for the shallot and pepper. Give everything a good mix and set aside for 10 minutes.

Mango salsa

Meanwhile, make the salsa. Add all the ingredients to a bowl, give it a good mix and set aside.

In a hot frying pan (skillet), add a drizzle of olive oil and fry the shallot and pepper for about 5 minutes.

Next, add the omelette mixture to the pan exactly as you would a traditional omelette and make sure it is evenly spread over the base. Fry for 5 minutes and then flip it over to cook the other side.

Get out a serving plate and transfer the omelette to it. Add one handful of rocket on one side, a spoonful or two of mango salsa, some sliced avocado, some spring onion and the pomegranate seeds, if using. You can choose to eat the omelette flat or fold it over on one side so that its shaped like a half moon. This recipe is best eaten and served immediately. Enjoy!

HOT SPICY CHOCOLATE WITH VANILLA

Who doesn't like to cosy up with a mug of hot chocolate on a cold evening, or morning for that matter? This version has a chilli kick and the added bonus of keeping as much goodness as possible in one cupful.

Makes 2 small cups or 1 large

80 g (3 oz / ½ cup) blanched (skinless) almonds (soaked for 30 minutes)
500 ml (17 fl oz / 2 cups) water
3 tablespoons cacao powder
1 tablespoon maple syrup
pinch of chilli powder
pinch of salt
1 vanilla pod (bean)

Add all the ingredients into a high-speed blender, including the vanilla pod. (I usually just chuck it in whole and chop it up, I don't bother taking out the seeds inside as I think it's a bit of a waste of the pod.) Blitz until you have a lovely milky, frothy chocolate consistency, then pour the mixture into a small saucepan.

Slowly heat the mixture with a whisk until it reaches the temperature you would like.

I like my hot chocolate piping hot!

BATCH COOKABLE

LASTS FOR +3 DAYS
IN THE FRIDGE

NUT-FREE IF YOU
USE COCONUT
MILK INSTEAD OF
ALMOND

SALTED CARAMEL
SMOOTHIE

This recipe is super simple and a great way to make use of your bananas – they are great smoothie bases! Even though this only serves one, I would double batch the recipe as you'll definitely want second...

Serves 1

1 frozen banana
250 ml (8 fl oz / 1 cup) Almond Milk, shop-bought or home-made (see page 139)
pinch of ground vanilla pod (bean)
2 medjool dates, stoned (pitted)
pinch of salt
1 teaspoon cacao powder

Add all the ingredients to a blender, except the cacao powder.

Blitz until everything is well incorporated.

Pour into a glass and sprinkle the cacao powder on top or use a sieve for an even dusting.

Tip

Never throw your bananas away. The spottier they are, the sweeter and the better they are for freezing and using as a base for smoothies. Make sure you peel them and bag them properly before you pop them in the freezer. I always go double on this recipe but that's just me.

BATCH COOKABLE

LASTS FOR +3 DAYS
IN THE FRIDGE

NUT-FREE

WARMING COCONUT CHAI TEA

This tea emphasises comfort and warmth. Growing up in Tanzania, right next door to Zanzibar, this chai tea recipe reminds me of home. It can be made into a bigger batch and enjoyed throughout the day. This recipe is a staple at home.

Makes 4 cups

1 tablespoon coconut oil
2 cardamom pods
1 cinnamon stick
2 whole black peppercorns
1 thumb-sized piece of fresh root ginger, grated
pinch of chilli flakes (red pepper flakes) or 1 dried chilli
½ vanilla pod (bean)
500 ml (17 fl oz / 2 cups) water
1 rooibos tea bag
500 ml (17 fl oz / 2 cups) coconut milk (preferably Tetra Pak, which is consistently creamy and doesn't separate)
1 tablespoon maple syrup

Start by heating the coconut oil in a medium saucepan, then add all the spices including the ginger, chilli and vanilla pod and gently heat for 5 minutes. Squash the cardamon pods first so that the seeds come out and you get their full flavour.

Add the water and rooibos tea bag, bring to the boil and boil for about 10 minutes.

After 10 minutes, turn it down to a simmer and add the coconut milk. Make sure the liquid heats up but keep it just at a simmer – if it boils, the milk and water will separate and the chai won't look very nice.

Once the mixture is warm, add your choice of sweetener.

Tip

You can keep the spice mix in the pan and just keep refilling the pan with water and coconut milk to make more batches of tea throughout the day. If you are spending the day at home, pottering about, this is the perfect drink to keep you warm.

HOME

ALONE

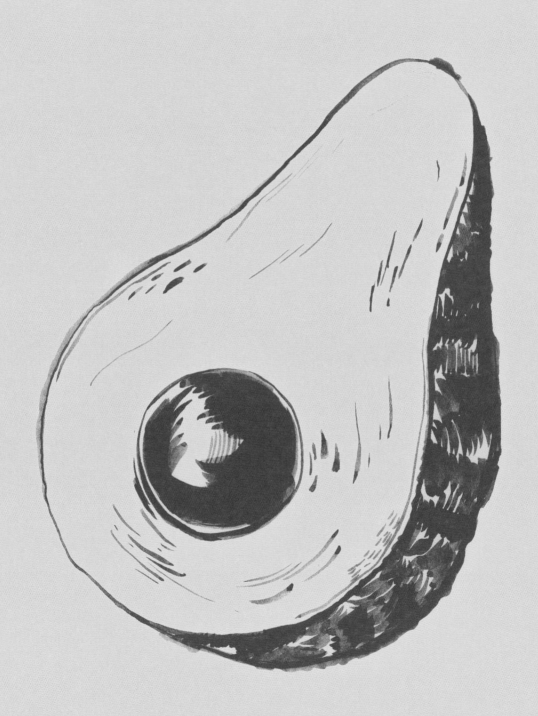

HOME ALONE

These are meals for households of one to two people that are easy peasy, satisfying and full of flavour. There are many times when cooking a meal from scratch when you get home after a long day at work can be the last thing on your to-do list, but what if I told you that it would take you as long to cook a meal for yourself as it would to call in a takeaway? This is food I like to eat: classics with a veggie twist. I have cooked these on numerous occasions and every time they make me feel warm and cosy on the inside. Simply happy! Just the way food should make you feel.

BATCH COOKABLE

FREEZABLE

LASTS FOR +5 DAYS
IN THE FRIDGE

NUT-FREE

AVOCADO ON TOAST THE BETTINA'S KITCHEN WAY

Avocados make me HAPPY! I am obsessed with them, they are nature's own bundle of nutrition. I also love the typical breakfast that is served all over Spain: *pan con tomate*, meaning bread with tomato. Truly it is a match made in heaven. This is my all-time favourite meal. I hope you love it as much as I do.

Serves 1

2 slices of Super Bread
   (see page 148) or good-quality
   shop-bought bread
½ avocado, sliced

For the tomato topping
(makes enough for 2–4 slices)
1 big ripe tomato or 2 small ones
1 teaspoon salt
pinch of black pepper
1 tablespoon apple cider vinegar
1 teaspoon maple syrup
½ garlic clove, peeled
3 tablespoons good olive oil

To serve
rocket (arugula)
watercress
basil
sesame seeds
hemp hearts
sprouts

Tomato topping Place all the tomato ingredients into a blender and blitz until everything is well combined, then set aside.

Pop the bread into a toaster and crisp up.

Place the toast on a plate and add a layer of tomato topping, sliced avocado and any of the serving options. I love topping my toast with rocket or watercress and basil and a sprinkling of seeds, hemp hearts or sprouts for added flavour and nutrition.

Tip Make sure you get good-quality tomatoes for this dish, you will taste the difference. The tomato topping can be stored in an airtight container in the fridge for up to 5 days. The bread can be frozen, but make sure you slice it first.

BATCH COOKABLE

FREEZABLE

+5 DAYS

LASTS FOR +5 DAYS
IN THE FRIDGE

ONE-POT CURRY IN A HURRY

Have you had a long day at work? Do you just want to chuck everything into a pot and let it cook itself? Then this is the dish for you. By the time you have put on your comfies and slippers this creamy, indulgent one-pot curry will be ready to be eaten.

Serves 2

2 tablespoons olive oil
1 shallot, finely chopped
1 garlic clove, peeled and chopped
1 tablespoon good-quality
   yellow curry spice mix,
   plus more if required
1 carrot, chopped into small pieces
½ aubergine (eggplant),
   chopped into small pieces
1 potato, chopped into small pieces
45 g (1½ oz / ¼ cup) dried red lentils
400 ml (14 fl oz / 1½ cups)
   coconut milk
1 tablespoon peanut butter
big handful of spinach
big bunch of basil
salt and pepper, to taste

To serve
pomegranate seeds
chopped peanuts
squeeze of lime
coriander (cilantro) leaves
edible flowers (optional)

Heat a frying pan (skillet) over medium heat. Add the oil and gently fry the shallot and garlic until transparent. Then add the curry spice mix, carrot, aubergine and potato and fry for another 5 minutes.

Stir in the lentils followed by the coconut milk and simmer over low heat, covered, for 25 minutes.

Remove the lid, taste and adjust the seasoning with salt or more spice mix, add a dollop of peanut butter and stir in a handful of spinach and basil. I also love to scatter over pomegranate seeds and peanuts for extra crunch and give it a final squeeze of lime to cut through the creaminess of the curry, then throw over a few coriander leaves and edible flowers, to add some colour.

Serve as it is or with some steamed rice, quinoa or buckwheat on the side.

Tip

Curries are great when cooked in bigger batches – often they taste even better the next day because the flavours have had a chance to marry.

BATCH COOKABLE

+3 DAYS

LASTS FOR +3 DAYS
IN THE FRIDGE

SPICY THAI NOODLES WITH CREAMY PEANUT DRESSING

Easy, spicy with an Asian flare. A great way to include as many vegetables as possible, masking them with a spicy sauce that will make anything taste amazing!

Serves 2

200 g (7 oz) rice noodles
1 carrot, julienned
¼ courgette (zucchini),
   cut into ribbons
¼ red (bell) pepper, julienned
¼ yellow (bell) pepper, julienned
¼ mango, julienned
1 spring onion (scallion), chopped
handful of spinach

For the peanut dressing
½ red chilli, finely chopped
a few sprigs of basil
½ lime
black sesame seeds
½ tablespoon finely grated
   fresh root ginger
3 tablespoons peanut butter
1 tablespoon maple syrup
1 teaspoon apple cider vinegar
80 ml (2½ fl oz / ⅓ cup) water
1 tablespoon tamari soy sauce

To serve
a few sprigs of mint
a few sprigs of basil or Thai basil
½ lime
black sesame seeds

	Cook the rice noodles following the packet instructions. Drain and set aside.
Peanut dressing	Mix all the dressing ingredients together in a bowl, and set aside.
	Combine all the prepared vegetables for the noodle dish in a big bowl. Add in the noodles and stir in the dressing so that everything gets coated.
	Serve in bowls sprinkled with the fresh herbs and with a lime wedge for squeezing over. Sprinkle over some black sesame seeds for a bit of extra crunch.
Tip	Great dish for making in advance – perfect as a lunch-box meal to take to work.

BATCH COOKABLE

LASTS FOR +3 DAYS
IN THE FRIDGE

PASTA PESTO & NUT PARMESAN

Fast food made well. This is one of the quickest meals in this book, and it's filling, comforting and everything else you want out of a bowl of pasta. Pasta is a staple food in our house and this dish will not disappoint.

Serves 2

200 g (7 oz) good-quality gluten-free pasta or your preference – such as spelt or wholegrain (I use spaghetti for this dish)
½ courgette (zucchini)
4 tablespoons Pumpkin Seed Pesto (see page 151)
4 tablespoons Nut Parmesan (see page 145)
handful of basil
handful of rocket (arugula)

Cook the pasta following the packet instructions.

While the pasta is cooking, cut the courgette into ribbons, either with a slicer or just roughly grate it, then set aside.

Drain the cooked pasta, reserving a tiny bit of the cooking water, then return the pasta to the saucepan.

Stir in the pumpkin seed pesto along with the courgette and give it a good stir until all the pasta is coated.

Ladle into bowls, top with the nut Parmesan, some basil and peppery rocket and serve straightaway. This is one of my go-to quick meals, especially after a long day.

Tip

Great lunch box meal or travel meal.

BATCH COOKABLE

FREEZABLE

4-5 DAYS

LASTS FOR 4-5 DAYS
IN THE FRIDGE

MY FAVOURITE QUINOA BOWL, VEGGIES, BEANS & BASIL MAYO

Quinoa is now a household staple. This little super seed has made its way onto our plates and is a great alternative to rice and other grains. I love eating it with other components and this recipe is one that I make again and again.

Serves 1

150 g (5 oz / ¾ cup) quinoa

**For the dressing
(makes a small 200 ml / 7 fl oz jar)**
125 ml (4 fl oz / ½ cup) olive oil
1 teaspoon Dijon mustard
1 teaspoon maple syrup
1 teaspoon salt
pinch of black pepper
½ shallot, very finely chopped
2 tablespoons apple cider vinegar

For the beans
150 g (5 oz) butter beans (lima beans), shop-bought or cooked
½ tomato, finely chopped
2 tablespoons chopped parsley
squeeze of lemon juice

For the basil mayo
125 g (4 oz / ½ cup) Cashew Yoghurt (see page 140)
handful of basil
pinch of salt

To serve
mixed greens
ribboned cucumber
fresh herbs (optional)

Cook the quinoa following the packet instructions and set aside.

Dressing   Add all the dressing ingredients to a jar, give it a good shake and set aside.

Beans   For the beans, add all the ingredients to a bowl, pour half of the prepared dressing over and give it a good stir.

Basil mayo   Put the basil mayo ingredients into a blender and blitz until you have a lovely smooth green mayo and set aside.

In a bowl, arrange the cooked quinoa and a generous spoonful of the beans. I like my bowl with a good helping of mixed greens and ribboned cucumber, too. Add a big dollop of the basil mayo on top and drizzle an extra helping of the dressing on the greens.

Tip   This dish can be made in bigger batches and is fantastic as a lunch box meal. The basil mayo will last for up to 4–5 days in the fridge and can also be made in larger amounts and frozen. The quinoa can also be cooked, frozen, and used as needed.

BATCH COOKABLE

FREEZABLE

LASTS FOR +3 DAYS
IN THE FRIDGE

NUT-FREE

MEXICAN BOWL – BLACK BEANS, GUACAMOLE & OVEN-ROASTED SWEET POTATOES

Mexican cuisine is an all-time favourite and one of those dishes that can easily be made to take on outings, picnics or for lunch in the office. Also, you probably know by now that I am a huge avocado fan!

Serves 2

2 tablespoons olive oil
1 shallot, chopped
¼ leek, finely chopped
1 garlic clove, peeled and chopped
220 g (8 oz / 2 cups) black beans from a tin or jar, drained
1 x 400 g (14 oz) tin chopped tomatoes
1 teaspoon cayenne pepper
1 teaspoon salt
1 square of dark chocolate, 90% cocoa solids

Oven-roasted sweet potato
400 g (14 oz) sweet potato, peeled and cut into chunks
sprig of thyme
pink Himalayan salt and black pepper, to taste
olive oil, for roasting

Guacamole
1 avocado, stoned (pitted)
¼ red onion, finely chopped
½ garlic clove, peeled and grated
juice of ½ lime
¼ mango, peeled and finely chopped

To serve
dollops of Coconut Yoghurt, shop-bought or home-made (see page 142)
sprinkle of coriander (cilantro) leaves
mixed leafy greens

Oven-roasted sweet potato

Preheat the oven to 200°C (400°F/Gas 6). Line a baking tray (baking sheet) with greaseproof paper (wax paper). Put the sweet potato chunks and sprig of thyme on the tray, sprinkle with salt and pepper to taste along with a good glug of olive oil and roast in the oven for 20–30 minutes, keeping an eye on them so that they don't burn.

Meanwhile, heat the olive oil in a medium pan and add the shallot, leek and garlic and gently brown. Add the black beans and give it a stir. Then add the tomatoes and cayenne and let the beans simmer for 20 minutes on a medium heat.

Guacamole

While the beans and potatoes are cooking, make the guacamole by mashing the avocado in a bowl. Add the rest of the ingredients with a pinch of salt and pepper, give a good stir and set aside.

Check on the beans. Once the liquid from the tomatoes has evaporated and you are left with a sticky smoky bean mixture, season with salt and pepper and drop in the square of dark chocolate, stirring it to melt.

Add a spoonful each of the bean mixture, sweet potatoes and guacamole into 2 serving bowls. I love mine with a good dollop of coconut yoghurt, a sprig or two of coriander and some leafy greens.

Tip

The black beans are freezable.

BATCH COOKABLE

FREEZABLE

LASTS FOR +3 DAYS IN THE FRIDGE

NUT-FREE

GARDEN VEGETABLE SOUP WITH FRESH HERBS

Another great one-pot meal. I love eating chunky vegetable soups, I so prefer them to the blitzed, smooth versions. This is a feel-good classic with an option to add in lots of fresh herbs at the end. I love this soup with dill and chopped parsley, but it is not always to everyone's liking, so serve the herbs separately for people to scatter over if they like.

Serves 1

a good glug of olive oil
1 yellow onion, sliced
1 garlic clove, peeled and chopped
1 carrot, finely chopped
1 bay leaf
½ red (bell) pepper, diced
¼ courgette (zucchini), diced
1 potato, diced
handful of frozen or fresh peas
500 ml (17 oz / 2 cups) water
handful of chopped kale
1 teaspoon salt
pinch of black pepper, to taste

To serve
1 teaspoon chopped dill
1 tablespoon chopped parsley
Super Bread (see page 148) or
  good-quality shop-bought bread

Heat the olive oil in a pan over medium heat and fry the onion, garlic and carrot until the onion is golden and the carrot is tender.

Add the bay leaf and the rest of the vegetables, except the kale. Add the water and let the soup simmer for 20 minutes until the vegetables are soft but not mushy.

Add seasoning to taste and stir in the chopped kale to wilt. Or add kale to the bottom of the serving bowls and ladle hot soup over it.

Serve immediately with the chopped herbs scattered on the side and a side of home-made bread or just as it is. This is by far one of my favourite ways of eating as many veggies as possible in one sitting!

BATCH COOKABLE

FREEZABLE

+3 DAYS

LASTS FOR +3 DAYS
IN THE FRIDGE

NUT-FREE

GARLIC & ONION FRIED RICE, FRESH SAMBAL & MASHED AVOCADO

The sambal recipe in this dish was handed down to me when I was running a retreat in Bali. It is one of many Balinese versions but it is my favourite. It lasts forever and awakens any dull dish that needs some extra oomph!

Serves 2

440 g (1 lb / 2 cups) brown rice
1 tablespoon coconut oil, for frying
2 garlic cloves, peeled and sliced
2 shallots, sliced

**For the sambal
(makes one 200 g / 7 oz jar)**
1 red Thai chilli
½ shallot
1 medjool date, stoned (pitted)
½ tablespoon salt
2 tablespoons grated fresh
    root ginger
1 garlic clove, peeled
1 tomato, deseeded and chopped
½ red (bell) pepper, deseeded
    and roughly chopped
1 tablespoon apple cider vinegar
squeeze of lime juice
60 ml (2 fl oz / ¼ cup) olive oil

For the sides
handful of tenderstem broccoli
    (broccolini)
handful of kale
a couple of pak choi (bok choy)
1 avocado, mashed until smooth

To serve
sesame seeds
peanuts
baby spinach
lime wedges

Cook the rice following the packet instructions. Drain.

Sambal Put all the sambal ingredients into a food processor and blitz until you get a sauce-like consistency. Pour into a jar or an airtight container that can easily be stored in the fridge. (This will keep for over a week in the fridge.)

Bring a medium saucepan of water to a boil and blanch the broccoli stems, kale and pak choi for a few minutes, remove with a slotted spoon and set aside on kitchen paper (paper towel).

Heat a large pan over medium heat and add the coconut oil, garlic and shallots and fry until golden brown. Add the cooked rice and stir-fry until all the ingredients are well combined and rice is slightly golden.

Divide between 2 bowls and top with a handful of the broccoli and kale and a dollop of avocado. Serve with a good dollop of fresh and zingy sambal and a sprinkling of sesame seeds. I love my bowl with an extra helping of baby spinach for added greens and a lime wedge for zing.

Tip Everything except for the mashed avocado can be frozen.

BATCH COOKABLE

FREEZABLE

LASTS FOR +3 DAYS
IN THE FRIDGE

NUT-FREE

KOREAN PANCAKE WITH SLICED ROOTS & CHILLI SWEET & SOUR TAMARI

One of my dearest friends, Soljee, is from South Korea, and I have spent quite a lot of time there. One of my favourite and quickest dishes to make is the Korean pancake – crispy on the outside and filled with veggie goodness on the inside, it is wonderful dipped in the best tamari dressing ever!

Makes 1 big pancake, serves 2

70 g (3 oz / ½ cup) Gluten-free
   Flour Mix (see page 146)
160 ml (5 fl oz / ⅔ cup) water
pinch of bicarbonate of soda
   (baking soda)
olive oil, for frying
100 g (3½ oz) asparagus spears
   (½ bunch), sliced lengthways
½ leek, sliced lengthways
1 carrot, chopped into thin sticks

For the dressing
60 ml (2 fl oz / ¼ cup) tamari
   soy sauce
juice of ½ lime
1 tablespoon sesame oil
1 teaspoon maple syrup
½ garlic clove, peeled and grated

To serve
2 spring onions (scallions), chopped
black or white sesame seeds
coriander (cilantro), optional

Dressing

Start off by mixing all the ingredients for the dressing in a small jar, pop the lid on, give it a shake and set aside.

In a bowl, mix the flour, water and bicarbonate of soda and set aside.

Heat some oil in a frying pan (skillet) over medium heat. Add all the veggies and fry for 5 minutes until brown.

Spread the veggies out evenly in the pan and pour over the batter until you have a big pancake. Cook for 5 minutes on each side until crispy and golden brown.

Serve immediately, cut into slices, topped off with the spring onions, sesame seeds, coriander and the amazing dressing alongside.

Tip

Such an easy dish to serve as a starter, sharing platter or quick solo meal after a long day at work.

BATCH COOKABLE

FREEZABLE

+3 DAYS

LASTS FOR +3 DAYS IN THE FRIDGE

NUT-FREE

MY MOTHER'S COMFORTING BEAN SOUP

This soup is something I remember having when I was growing up. My grandmother was an amazing cook and passed on her skills to my mother, who in turn would make this particular soup during a Bulgarian holiday called *Badni Vecher*. It is a pre-Christmas tradition that has stuck with me ever since.

Serves 2

olive oil, for frying
1 small onion, finely chopped
½ green (bell) pepper, finely chopped
1 small carrot, finely chopped
1 tablespoon tomato purée (paste) or 3 tablespoons chopped tomatoes (it's just for taste)
1 teaspoon coconut sugar
400 g (14 oz) butter beans (lima beans), shop-bought or cooked
2 teaspoons paprika
½ tablespoon chopped parsley
½ tablespoon chopped thyme
1 teaspoon dried mint
500 ml (17 fl oz / 2 cups) water
pink Himalayan salt and black pepper, to taste

To serve
Super Bread (see page 148) or good-quality shop-bought bread, optional
a handful of rocket (arugula), optional

In a medium pan, heat some olive oil and fry the onion, pepper and carrot until nice and soft.

Next add in the tomato purée or tomatoes, coconut sugar, beans and all the spices and herbs and give it a good stir.

Add the water and gently simmer, covered, for 20 minutes.

Ladle out one helping of the bean soup into a bowl and mash the beans until you get a fine paste. Return the bean paste back into the pan – this will thicken it up and make it nice and creamy – and warm through, stirring.

Ladle the soup into bowls, top with rocket and enjoy with some lovely home-made bread on the side.

Tip

Great staple soup to make a big batch of and enjoy over a few days. I even think it tastes better the next day, once the ingredients have had a chance to marry.

BAKED SHAKSHUKA WITH BUTTER BEANS

Love this dish! So simple, satisfying and easy to make. The eggy version of shakshuka has taken over cafes worldwide. This version is still as substantial and has a spicy, smoky edge to it that I love.

Serves 2

80 ml (2½ fl oz / ⅔ cup) olive oil
½ red onion, chopped
½ red (bell) pepper, chopped
½ aubergine (eggplant), chopped
1 x 400 g (4 oz) tin of tomatoes
230 g (8 oz) tinned butter beans
  (lima beans), drained
4 sundried tomatoes, chopped
½ teaspoon sweet paprika
pinch of cayenne pepper
pink Himalayan salt and black
  pepper, to taste

To serve
handful of chopped parsley
Super Bread (see page 148) or
  good-quality shop-bought bread
drizzle of Pumpkin Seed Pesto
  (see page 151)
dollops of plant yoghurt,
  shop-bought or home-made
  (see pages 140 and 142)
lemon wedges
a few cherry tomatoes, to garnish
  (optional)
a few endive leaves, to garnish
  (optional)

In a medium pan, heat the oil and fry the onion, pepper and aubergine with a tiny pinch of salt for 10–15 minutes. It is important you use a good amount of oil here to get it going and to make sure that the veggies soften properly.

Then add the tomatoes, beans, sundried tomatoes and all the spices and seasoning, give it a good stir and leave on a medium heat, covered, for 10 minutes.

Check on the mixture when the time is up, give it a stir and leave for another 10 minutes.

By now the shakshuka should be done, the liquid should have mostly cooked off and turned sticky and there should be a smoky gorgeous mixture in your pan.

Serve immediately from the pan with a good sprinkle of chopped parsley, avocado slices, home-made bread for dipping and if you have some pumpkin seed pesto, get that in too, along with some plant yoghurt and lemon wedges to squeeze over.

Tip

This is such a comforting dish that can also be made in bigger quantities and reheated. It's a weekend brunch kind of meal, but also super when you're coming home from work and are in need of something substantial. I sometimes add some sliced avocado to mine, for extra creaminess, which I'm sure will come as no surprise!

BATCH COOKABLE

NUT-FREE

EPIC VEGGIE SANDWICH

I love a good sandwich – the more fillers, the better – and this veggie sandwich is no exception. We all lead busy lives, meaning that sometimes fast food is the solution. It doesn't get quicker and tastier than this. Crunchy, fresh, tart, salty and delicious.

Makes 2 sandwiches

2 slices of red onion
2 slices of tomato
2 slices of yellow (bell) pepper
2 lettuce leaves
4 slices of Super Bread
  (see page 148) or good-quality
  shop-bought bread
2 tablespoons Pumpkin Seed Pesto
  (see page 151), optional

For the ultimate hummus
200 g (7 oz / 1½ cups) tinned
  chickpeas, drained
3 tablespoons light tahini
juice of 1 lemon
5 tablespoons water
½ garlic clove, peeled
1 beetroot, chopped
1 teaspoon Dijon mustard
1 tablespoon capers, chopped
pink Himalayan salt and black
  pepper, to taste

Prepare all the veggies that are going into your epic sandwich and set aside.

Ultimate hummus
For the hummus, add all the ingredients to a blender and blitz until you have a lovely smooth texture, then set aside.

Now get 2 pieces of bread and spread them with pumpkin seed pesto (if using) and top with the hummus. Layer with veggies in between. Add a sprinkle of salt and pepper to taste before adding the top of the sandwich and giving it a good squeeze.

This is not date food – it is messy, gooey and absolutely yummy!

Tip
The hummus is a great standby ingredient and will last for up to a week, covered, in the fridge. Add it to bowl food, toast or use it as a dip.

QUICK &

SIMPLE

QUICK & SIMPLE

I am a practical kind of cook, and despite my love affair with food I don't always have a lot of time to spend in the kitchen. I like to prepare recipes in batches and keep in the fridge so that I can easily have access to good home-made food at any given time! If that's you, too, give these short and easy recipes a go. These are meals that are full of flavour with the added benefit of being super-quick to make. Inspired by my travels, these dishes have maximum flavour and as many veggies as possible crammed into one meal.

MAN-FLU SOUP WITH NOODLES, GINGER, GARLIC, ONIONS & LOTS OF SPICE

This soup was created for all of you who suffer immensely during flu season, as well as for those who just enjoy a bowl of comfort. Full of flavour, comforting and filling, this is a winner.

Serves 2

200 g (7 oz) rice noodles
olive oil, for cooking
1 shallot, sliced
3 shiitake mushrooms,
   dried or fresh
60 ml (2 fl oz / ¼ cup) tamari
   soy sauce
1 teaspoon coconut sugar
500 ml (17 fl oz / 2 cups) water
¼ daikon (Asian radish), diced
1 pak choi (bok choy),
   cut lengthways
handful of sugar snap peas
   (snow peas)
½ garlic clove, peeled
1 big thumb-sized piece of fresh
   root ginger

To serve
spring onions (scallions)
freshly chopped red chilli (optional)
coriander (cilantro) leaves
lime wedges

Start by cooking the rice noodles following the packet instructions, drain and set aside.

In a medium pan heat the oil and add the shallot and shiitake mushrooms. If you are using dried shiitake make sure you have soaked them for at least 30 minutes in hot water and drain them properly before use. Cook for about 5 minutes, then add the tamari and coconut sugar and take off the heat.

Put the pan back on the heat and add the water, daikon, pak choi and sugar snaps. Turn up the heat and bring to the boil.

Once the soup has started boiling, take off the heat, grate in the garlic, then add the ginger. I learnt a great trick from a fellow foodie: grate the ginger onto a chopping board, then take it in your hand and squeeze the juice out into the soup. That way you get good-quality juice and flavour without any bits.

Prepare 2 bowls, add the noodles to each and pour over the hot soup broth, then sprinkle with spring onions, chilli for heat, if using, and coriander and serve with lime wedges for squeezing.

BATCH COOKABLE

+3
DAYS

LASTS FOR +3 DAYS
IN THE FRIDGE

JUICY TOMATO
SPAGHETTI &
NON-MEATBALLZ

Who doesn't love a good bowl of spaghetti?
I know I do, and when it is as simple as this to
prepare there's no excuse not to give it a go.

Serves 2

200 g (7 oz) gluten-free pasta
 or other good-quality pasta
1 batch of The Best Non-meatballz
 Ever (see page 154)

For the sauce
olive oil, for frying
1 small carrot, diced
1 small shallot, diced
½ small courgette (zucchini), diced
1 x 400 g (14 oz) tin tomatoes or
 good-quality tomato sauce
pink Himalayan salt and black
 pepper, to taste
bunch of basil, plus extra to serve

To serve
Nut Parmesan (see page 145)
basil and rocket (arugula) leaves

Sauce

Heat the oil in a medium pan and add all the chopped veggies. Flavour with a pinch of salt
and fry until nice and soft, about 10 minutes.

Add the chopped tomatoes or tomato sauce to the pan, cover with a lid and simmer for
20 minutes.

Meanwhile, cook the pasta following the packet instructions.

Once the sauce has reduced and thickened, gently stir in a handful of basil. Drain the pasta,
add it to the sauce and give it another gentle stir. At this stage you can add the non-meatballz
and warm through.

Serve straight from the pan sprinkled with nut Parmesan and a handful of basil.

BATCH COOKABLE

FREEZABLE

LASTS FOR +3 DAYS
IN THE FRIDGE

HAZELNUT CRUST PIZZA & PEPPERY ROCKET

I love a good pizza! But it's one of the big no-nos when going gluten-free. I have made this at countless retreats and on many occasions at home. I hope you love it as much as I do.

Serves 2–4

For the pizza base
210 g (7½ oz / 1½ cups) Gluten-free Flour Mix (see page 146)
30 g (1 oz / ¼ cup) hazelnuts, ground in a coffee grinder or food processor
375 ml (13 fl oz / 1½ cups) water
½ teaspoon bicarbonate of soda (baking soda)
½ teaspoon salt
2 tablespoons olive oil, plus extra for greasing

For the toppings
4 tablespoons Pumpkin Seed Pesto (see page 151)
1 red onion, sliced
25 g (1 oz / ¼ cup) chopped sundried tomatoes
a handful of cherry tomatoes, halved
½ red (bell) pepper, sliced
½ yellow (bell) pepper, sliced
pink Himalayan salt and black pepper, to taste

To serve
basil
rocket (arugula)
drizzle of olive oil
micro herbs (optional)
Macadamia Ricotta (see page 144), optional, but recommended for special occasions

Pizza base

Preheat the oven to 200°C (400°F/Gas 6). Add all the pizza base ingredients to a bowl and mix well. The mixture will be quite runny, almost like a cake batter. Don't worry, it's meant to be that way.

Line a baking tray (baking sheet) with greaseproof paper (wax paper) and drizzle a very small amount of olive oil on the bottom. Pour the pizza batter into the tray and make sure you have a thin, even layer.

Topping

Cook in the oven for 15 minutes until the the dough has solidified. Once it has, take it out of the oven and it's ready to be pimped up with toppings. I love this base with a layer of the pumpkin seed pesto and scatterings of red onion, sundried tomato, cherry tomatoes and peppers. Add your toppings and put the pizza back in the oven for another 15 minutes until it reaches the desired crispness.

Just before serving, scatter a good helping of basil, rocket and extra drizzle of olive oil and salt and pepper. If you have some macadamia ricotta ready-made, add some nice dollops of it on top, too.

Tip

You can pre-make the pizza base. Get to the stage where you cooked the base in the oven, then wrap it up in greaseproof paper (wax paper) or cling film (plastic wrap) and freeze until you need it. All you need to do when you feel like pizza is top it off with your favourite toppings and pop it into the oven!

BATCH COOKABLE

NUT-FREE

POLENTA WITH OVEN-ROASTED TOMATOES & SWEET, STICKY GARLIC

I have eaten polenta in many versions and in different countries. There is something about the combination of garlic and roasted tomato that is very hard to beat. Another easy recipe that will warm your heart.

Serves 2

14 cherry tomatoes on the vine
olive oil, for cooking
pink Himalayan salt
1 teaspoon coconut sugar

For the sweet sticky garlic
1 shallot, sliced
2 garlic cloves, peeled and sliced
1 teaspoon sweet paprika
1 teaspoon maple syrup
2 tablespoons walnuts, chopped

For the polenta base
1 shallot, sliced
½ red (bell) pepper, sliced
70 g (2½ oz / ⅓ cup) polenta
500 ml (17 fl oz / 2 cups) water
250 ml (8½ fl oz / 1 cup) plant milk
    (for extra creaminess, use coconut)

To serve
rocket (arugula)
basil

Preheat the oven to 220°C (430°F/Gas 7) and line a baking tray (baking sheet) with greaseproof paper (wax paper). Put the cherry tomatoes on the tray, drizzle with olive oil and sprinkle with 1 teaspoon of salt and coconut sugar. Roast in the oven for 20 minutes.

Sweet sticky garlic

In a medium pan, heat some olive oil and fry the shallot and garlic for about 5 minutes. Flavour with salt and sweet paprika and give it a stir. When the shallots have softened, add the maple syrup and pine nuts and set aside.

Polenta base

Next, make the polenta base. Heat some olive oil in a pan and fry the shallots and red pepper until soft, about 5 minutes.

Add the polenta and water to a medium pan and give it a stir on a medium heat. The mixture will start to bubble and thicken. Thin it out with your plant milk of choice. I like using coconut because it is thick, but any type will do.

Once you have a lovely creamy consistency, take the pan off the heat. Spoon out the polenta onto plates and decorate with the roasted tomatoes, sweet sticky topping and a handful of rocket and basil.

BATCH COOKABLE

FREEZABLE

+3
DAYS

LASTS FOR +3 DAYS
IN THE FRIDGE

SWEET POTATO CAKES WITH DILL & CASHEW YOGHURT

What can I say? This is one of my favourite recipes. It reminds me of the many fishcakes I used to have in Scandinavia growing up, and it includes a creamy, tangy dill dressing. Comforting on a whole other level!

Makes 4 cakes, serves 2

For the dill cashew yoghurt
125 ml (4 fl oz / ½ cup) Cashew Yoghurt (see page 140) or any plant yoghurt
1 tablespoon olive oil
1 tablespoon lemon juice
1 tablespoon chopped dill
1 tablespoon chopped capers
pink Himalayan salt and black pepper, to taste

For the sweet potato cakes
2 sweet potatoes (500 g / 1 lb 2 oz), peeled and cut into chunks
1 shallot, finely diced
1 red chilli, finely chopped
½ (70 g / 2½ oz) apple, finely chopped
40 g (1½ oz / ⅓ cup) cornflour (cornstarch)
coconut oil or grapeseed oil (both are good for high-temperature cooking), for frying

To serve
watercress or spinach
rocket (arugula)
mixed greens

Dill cashew yoghurt	To make the dill cashew yoghurt – add all the ingredients to a bowl and mix well, then set aside in the fridge until later.
Sweet potato cakes	Boil the sweet potatoes in a pan of water until soft, then tip into a colander and leave to drain for 10 minutes until really dry.
	In a bowl, mash the drained potatoes with a fork or masher, but don't overmash them or they will become glutinous and too sticky.
	Add the shallot, chilli, apple, salt and pepper to taste and finally the cornflour. Portion the mixture into 4 big cakes or 6 smaller ones and shape into round, flat-faced burgers.
	In a medium pan, add some oil and get it very hot, then fry the cakes for 5–10 minutes on each side until golden brown. You will be tempted to keep flipping them, but don't. Let one side cook first before flipping and cooking the other side.
	Drain on greaseproof paper (wax paper) or kitchen towel (paper towel) and serve with a good dollop of the dill yoghurt and some fresh greens.
Tip	If you do not want to fry the potato cakes, you can easily cook them in the oven at 200°C (400°F/Gas 6) for 20 minutes or until golden brown. The sweet potato cakes and yoghurt are both freezable.

BATCH COOKABLE

FREEZABLE

LASTS FOR +3 DAYS
IN THE FRIDGE

NUT-FREE

MARIO'S ITALIAN STUFFED VEGGIES

A steady favourite in the Bordi family. My larger-than-life Italian father-in-law makes these wonderful stuffed veggies on visits.

Serves 2

2 aubergines (eggplants)
1 courgette (zucchini)
2 (bell) peppers – 1 yellow, 1 red
1 big tomato
1 red onion or 2 small shallots, finely chopped
2 handfuls of parsley (60 g / 2½ oz), finely chopped
15 g (½ oz / ¼ cup) gluten-free breadcrumbs
pinch of salt and pepper, to taste
good drizzle of olive oil

To serve
drizzle of Pumpkin Seed Pesto (see page 151)
basil

Preheat the oven to 240°C (450°F/Gas 8).

While the oven is heating up, cut all of the vegetables, except the onion, in half and scooping out the insides. Place the scooped-out flesh of the aubergines and courgette into a bowl, but discard the insides of the tomato and peppers. Be careful not to scoop out too much. A note on aubergines: if they are big and a bit older the seeds can get bitter, so make sure you taste the mixture before you cook it.

Add the red onion and parsley to the bowl along with the breadcrumbs, salt and pepper to taste and a good glug of olive oil – don't be stingy! Give it a good mix.

Line a baking tray (baking sheet) with greaseproof paper (wax paper) and drizzle olive oil on the bottom. Arrange the vegetable shells on the tray and divide the filling equally among them.

Cook in the oven for 15 minutes then turn the temperature down to 180°C (350°F/Gas 4) and cook for another 30 minutes until the vegetables have got a lovely crisp top and look nice and soft on the inside.

Serve immediately with drizzles of pesto and a handful of fresh basil. This dish goes so well with bread, steamed quinoa or rice, or as one of many dishes when feasting.

BATCH COOKABLE

FREEZABLE

LASTS FOR +3 DAYS
IN THE FRIDGE

COURGETTE & PEPPER ROSTIS WITH CHIPOTLE MAYO, AVOCADO & CARAMELISED ONIONS

Even though this recipe has a few components, it's really easy peasy. Once you have put this dish together you will have an element of spice, some crunch from the rostis and some tang from the lime. Great for brunch or even as a starter for a dinner party.

Serves 2–4

For the caramelised onions
3 tablespoons olive oil
1 big onion, chopped into thin half moons
1 tablespoon maple syrup
pinch of pink Himalayan salt and black pepper

For the chipotle mayo
110 g (3¾ oz / ½ cup) Cashew Yoghurt (see page 140) or any plant yoghurt
1 teaspoon chipotle chilli paste or 1 small dried chilli
squeeze of lemon

For the rosti
2 large courgettes (zucchini) (400 g / 14 oz)
2 tablespoons flaxseeds
60 ml (2 fl oz / ¼ cup) water
20 g (¾ oz / ⅓ cup) gluten-free breadcrumbs
¼ leek, thinly sliced lengthways
1 small red (bell) pepper, sliced thinly lengthways
coconut oil or grapeseed oil, for frying
½ teaspoon cayenne pepper
salt and pepper, to taste

To serve
1 avocado, sliced
coriander (cilantro)
mixed greens
sprouts
lime wedges

Caramelised onions

In a medium pan, heat the olive oil, then add the onion and let it slow-cook for 10–15 minutes until soft.

Add salt and pepper to taste and finish off by adding the maple syrup to get the final sticky effect while it is still warm. Set aside.

Chipotle mayo

Make the mayo by adding all the ingredients to a bowl and mix well. Set aside.

Rosti

Next prepare the rosti. Grate the courgettes and sprinkle some salt over them. Allow to sit for about 20 minutes. In the meantime, prepare the flax egg by blending the flaxseeds with the water and leave to sit for 10–20 minutes until you get a gelatinous texture. This is the plant-based egg replacer.

Put the courgettes in a large, clean tea towel and squeeze out any excess water. Tip into a large bowl then add the breadcrumbs, leek, red pepper, flax egg, salt and pepper. Mix well.

Form the rosti mixture into flat-faced patties about the size of your palm and press gently to flatten.

Heat the oil in a large pan over medium heat. Cook the rosti until golden, about 5 minutes on each side, then flip and cook for another few minutes on the other side until nicely browned and crisped up.

Serve with the sliced avocado, a dollop of chipotle mayo, the caramelised onions and some coriander, mixed greens and a lime wedge.

Tip

This recipe can be prepped in advance and cooked just before serving. Very practical if you are having guests over or you would like to have a fancy savoury brunch.

BATCH COOKABLE

FREEZABLE

+3 DAYS

LASTS FOR +3 DAYS
IN THE FRIDGE

NUT-FREE

BIBIMBAP – KOREAN RICE BOWL WITH ALL THE SIDES

A bowl with different components that become the tastiest combination. Another Korean favourite that is easy to make and satisfying for the taste buds. I have also made this as a takeaway meal on several occasions.

Serves 2

440 g (1 lb / 2¼ cups) white rice

For the sautéed red cabbage
1 shallot, chopped in half moons
olive oil, for frying
½ head of red cabbage, thinly sliced
1 tablespoon tamari soy sauce
1 tablespoon maple syrup

For the marinated carrots
2 carrots, grated
1 tablespoon apple cider vinegar
1 tablespoon toasted sesame oil
1 tablespoon black sesame seeds
squeeze of lime

For the sweet & sour dressing
80 ml (2½ fl oz / ⅓ cup) tamari
  soy sauce
1 tablespoon toasted sesame oil
1 tablespoon maple syrup
1 small spring onion
  (scallion), chopped
½ chilli, chopped

For the griddled asparagus
150 g (5 oz) asparagus
½ garlic clove, peeled and grated
olive oil

To serve
extra greens, such as watercress

Cook the rice following the packet instructions.

Sautéed red cabbage

While the rice is cooking, get started on the cabbage. Add the shallot to a medium pan with the olive oil and fry for 5 minutes. Then add the red cabbage and fry on a medium heat for at least 20 minutes, stirring.

After 20 minutes the cabbage should have softened. Add the tamari and maple syrup and cook for another 10 minutes. Once it has a lovely sticky consistency take off the heat and set aside.

Marinated carrots

Put all the carrot ingredients into a bowl. Give it a good mix and set aside.

Sweet & sour dressing

Mix all the dressing ingredients together. I like to use small jar when making dressings so that I can give it a good shake and minimise mess.

Griddled asparagus

Last but not least, marinate the asparagus with the grated garlic, covered with olive oil, for 10 minutes before frying. Then fry in a medium pan until nice and crisp on the outside.

Serve the dish while the asparagus is hot. The best way to put this dish together is by getting a bowl out and adding a big spoonful of each ingredient. Serve the dressing in a small bowl or ramekin alongside. In South Korea this dish is eaten by adding the dressing to your food and mixing all the ingredients together well on the plate.

Tip

This is such a good weekly prep dish. Just double the amounts, store them in separate containers in the fridge and build your bibimbap bowls during the week. I would always suggest freshly cooking the rice when needed just because it tastes so much better.

BATCH COOKABLE

FREEZABLE

+3
DAYS

LASTS FOR +3 DAYS
IN THE FRIDGE

LOADED TACOS, WALNUT MINCE & APPLE WASABI SLAW

Tacos have been a firm favourite in our household for a long time. I also know that they bring an element to familiarity to the table, along with comfort. This is my 'when in doubt' recipe, which is especially for clients or dinner guests who are weary of plant-based foods.

Makes 4–6 loaded taco shells, serves 2–4

4–6 good-quality, shop-bought taco shells or tortillas

For the slaw
½ red cabbage
1 red apple, cut in half and cored
1 tablespoon maple syrup
1 tablespoon capers, chopped
1 tablespoon wasabi paste
2 tablespoons apple cider vinegar

For the walnut mince
150 g (5 oz / ¾ cup) quinoa
1 red onion, sliced
2 garlic cloves, peeled and sliced
olive oil, for frying
220 g (8 oz / 1 cup) walnuts, chopped
1 tablespoon fajita spice mix or taco spice
1 tablespoon tomato purée (paste)
salt and pepper, to taste

To serve
cherry tomatoes (optional)
coriander (cilantro)
dollop of Cashew Yoghurt (see page 140), or any plant yoghurt
lime wedges

Preheat the oven to 200°C (400°F/Gas 6).

Cook the quinoa following the packet instructions and set aside.

Slaw

Start the slaw. Thinly slice the red cabbage and apple on a mandolin or grater and add to a bowl. Add the rest of the ingredients and some seasoning, then give it a good mix and massage with your hands. Set aside.

Walnut mince

In a hot pan, add the red onion and garlic and fry in the olive oil until the onions are soft, about 5 minutes.

Add the chopped walnuts, quinoa, spices and tomato purée and cook for another 10 minutes over a medium heat until all the ingredients are well incorporated.

Once the mince is done, pop the tacos or tortillas into the oven for 5 minutes. Put the warmed tacos or tortillas on a serving plate and load up with slaw, mince, optional cherry tomatoes, coriander, yoghurt and lime wedges for squeezing over.

This dish is the nuts – so good, so satisfying, and both the slaw and mince can be made ahead and just put together before serving.

Tip

The walnut mince is freezable.

FEASTS &

SHARING

FEASTS& SHARING

Feasts and sharing platters are my favourite. When eating plant-based it is so important to add variety to your plate in the form of textures, flavours, combinations and, last but not least, eye candy! After all, we feast with our eyes first, don't we? Many of the platters have been featured at retreats I've run all over the world and they are there to satisfy even the fussiest of eaters. (I'm talking about the husbands who are usually dragged along to those yoga and meditation retreats!) Sharing meals together is so important nowadays, especially when life tends to be as busy as it is.

BEETROOT QUINOA, MACADAMIA RICOTTA & ORANGE DRESSING

A brightly coloured, bound to impress salad platter. Another favourite eaten on a hot summer's day or when wanting and needing a more substantial salad.

Serves 4

1 batch Macadamia Ricotta
  (see page 144)
lemon juice, to taste
salt and pepper, to taste

For coating the cheese
1 tablespoon mint
1 tablespoon parsley
1 tablespoon basil
pink Himalayan salt and black
  pepper, to taste

For the beetroot quinoa
4 small beetroots (beets)
440 g (1 lb / 2¼ cups) quinoa

For the salad
mixed baby salad leaves
2 oranges, sliced
bunch of mint leaves
Big Batch Dressing (see page 152)

Use a fresh batch of macadamia ricotta or let it ferment for a day. (The difference between leaving it to ferment or not is the added benefits of the probiotics and the acidic 'cheesy' taste it gets from the fermentation process.) Then add salt, pepper and lemon juice to the cheese until you have a good balance between salty and acidic.

Roll out a big piece of cling film (plastic wrap) and add all your cheese mixture to it – you can choose whether you would like a skinny cheese roll or a bigger one. I always find it is nicer to have bite-sized pieces, meaning a skinnier and longer cheese sausage. Once rolled, let it set in the fridge for an hour.

After an hour, or when it has set, unwrap the 'sausage' from the cling film.

Chop all the herbs on a chopping board or plate, and roll the nut cheese sausage in them, then slice into discs.

Beetroot quinoa

Put the beetroots in a big pan of water with a pinch of salt and let them boil for about an hour until soft. Cool, then purée in a blender until smooth. Set aside.

Cook the quinoa according to the packet instructions. Make sure you don't use too much water. I like using the ratio of 1 cup of quinoa to 1 cup of water. I start by letting the water boil, then add the quinoa, put the temperature right down, cover and cook until all the water has disappeared. Once the quinoa is fluffy and ready, set aside to cool.

Once cool, gently fold the beetroot purée into the pan until all of the quinoa has been covered.

Salad

Put together the salad by plating the salad leaves and topping with the beetroot quinoa, the orange slices, mint leaves, sliced herbed nut cheese and drizzle with zesty big batch dressing.

Tip

The macadamia ricotta is freezable.

BATCH COOKABLE

+14 DAYS

LASTS FOR +14
DAYS IN THE FRIDGE,
ESPECIALLY IF
GOING FOR THE
AGING.

TRUFFLED CASHEW CHEESE & CARAMELISED PEARS WITH SEEDED CRACKERS

My prized recipe. The closest I will get to the taste of cheese, and it also includes another favourite ingredient – the truffle. If you have the patience, do follow the aging process for the cheese – it takes 5–7 days, but it is so worth it.

Makes 2 Camembert-like rounds, serves 4

For the seeded crackers
85 g (3 oz / ½ cup) sesame seeds
85 g (3 oz / ½ cup) flaxseeds
65 g (2¼ oz / ½ cup) pumpkin seeds
65 g (2¼ oz / ½ cup) sunflower seeds
250 ml (8½ fl oz / 1 cup) water
30 g (1 oz / ¼ cup) Gluten-free Flour Mix (see page 146)

For the truffled cheese
1 batch Cashew Cheese (see page 146)
olive oil, for frying and greasing
1 shallot, finely chopped
juice of ½ lemon
1 tablespoon truffle oil
pink Himalayan salt and black pepper, to taste

For the caramelised pears
olive oil, for frying
2 pears, sliced
1 tablespoon maple syrup

Preheat the oven to 180°C (350°F/Gas 4).

Seeded crackers

Combine all the cracker ingredients except the flour in a bowl and let sit for 30 minutes. When the seeds have soaked up all the water, add the flour mix and give it a good stir. Line a baking tray (baking sheet) with greaseproof paper (wax paper) and spoon out the mixture and, using a spatula or spoon, even it out on the tray. Sprinkle with salt and pepper to taste and cook in the oven for 10 minutes. Take the crackers out of the oven and mark out perfect squares on the warm dough with a sharp knife, but don't cut them through completely, just enough so that it is easy to separate them later.

Put the crackers back in the oven and bake for another 20 minutes until they are cooked through and dry.

Truffled cheese

In a pan, add olive oil and the shallot and fry for 5 minutes until lovely and soft, then take off the heat. Grab the cheese mix from the fridge and add the shallot, lemon and truffle oil, season with salt and pepper and give it a good mix. This can now be eaten straight away as a cream cheese or aged into 2 round-shaped 'Camembert'-like cheeses.

If you are going to age your cheese, get a metal ring and grease it with olive oil on the inside. Place it on greaseproof paper on a flat surface (a small chopping board or a plate). Pile in the cheese mixture up to the top, then flatten.

Store in the fridge, uncovered, for 5–7 days until the cheese has produced a natural rind. At this point, gently remove the metal ring – it's ready to eat.

Caramelised pears

In a medium pan, heat some olive oil and add the pear slices. Cook them for 5 minutes on each side until beautiful and golden.

Just before taking the pan off the heat, add the maple syrup and a sprinkle of black pepper. I love creating a proper 'cheese board' by serving the pears and the crackers with the cheese.

BATCH COOKABLE

FREEZABLE

+3 DAYS

LASTS FOR +3 DAYS
IN THE FRIDGE

MARINATED MAPLE & TURMERIC-ROASTED CAULIFLOWER WITH YOGHURT SAUCE

I have to be honest, I am not a big fan of cauliflower but, if I were to eat it, this would be the version I would love the most!

Serves 2 as a main, 4 as a side

80 ml (2½ fl oz / ⅓ cup) olive oil
2 tablespoons maple syrup
1 tablespoon ground turmeric
pink Himalayan salt and black
 pepper, to taste
1 big whole cauliflower head
 or 2 small, broken into
 bite-sized florets

For the yoghurt sauce
80 g (3 oz / ⅓ cup) Cashew
 Yoghurt (see page 140)
 or any plant yoghurt
1 teaspoon chopped mint
1 tablespoon chopped coriander
 (cilantro)
juice of ½ lemon

To serve
handful of watercress or endive
handful of pomegranate seeds

Preheat the oven to 180°C (350°F/Gas 4).

In a bowl combine the oil, maple syrup, turmeric and seasoning. Tip the florets into the mix and give it a good stir. Make sure every floret is covered. Place on a baking tray (baking sheet) and cook in the oven for 30 minutes – check it every 10 minutes to make sure it doesn't burn.

Yoghurt sauce   Meanwhile, prepare the yoghurt sauce by mixing all the ingredients together. Set aside.

Once the cauliflower is cooked, tip it into a bowl, add the watercress or endive, sprinkle over the pomegranate seeds and drizzle dollops of refreshing yoghurt sauce on top.

Tip   The cauliflower is freezable.

BATCH COOKABLE

FREEZABLE

+5 DAYS

LASTS FOR +5 DAYS
IN THE FRIDGE

NUT-FREE

SWEDISH NON-MEATBALLZ, CARROT MASH, GRAVY & NAN'S QUICK PICKLE

My passport is Danish, my father Norwegian and I grew up in Sweden. I have been influenced by Scandinavian culture and flavours my whole life. This is an old Swedish classic with a plant-based twist, topped off with my grandmother's quick pickle. Truly, this is comfort in a bowl.

Serves 4

1 batch of The Best Non-meatballz
  Ever (see page 154)

For the quick pickle
1 cucumber
125 ml (4 fl oz / ½ cup) apple
  cider vinegar
3 tablespoons maple syrup
a pinch of salt
1 tablespoon chopped dill

For the carrot mash
6 large carrots, peeled
125 ml (4 fl oz / ½ cup)
  coconut milk
pink Himalayan salt and
  black pepper, to taste

For the gravy
olive oil, for frying
1 shallot, diced
2 tablespoons tamari soy sauce
1 tablespoon Maizena cornflour
  (cornstarch)
1 teaspoon coconut sugar
375 ml (13 fl oz / 1½ cups)
  coconut milk

To serve
mixed greens
lingonberries (optional)

Quick pickle	First make the pickle. Slice the cucumber thinly on a mandolin or use a cheese slicer. Add the slices to a bowl, then the rest of the ingredients. Give it a good mix and set aside.
Carrot mash	Next, make the carrot mash. In a large pan, boil the carrots until soft, then drain. Add to the blender with the coconut milk and blitz until you get the most beautiful orange mash. Add salt and pepper to taste.
Gravy	For the gravy, heat the olive oil and fry the shallots until nice and soft, about 5 minutes. Add the tamari, cornflour and sugar. Take off the heat and slowly add the coconut milk, a little at a time, to create a roux, whisking to avoid lumps.
	Put the pan back on the heat and let it simmer for 5 minutes until you have a lovely shiny gravy, then set aside.
	Now let's put everything together. Put the mash on a plate, followed by the gravy, then the meatballs and serve with quick pickles, mixed greens and, if you have them, some lingonberries.
Tip	If you don't know where to get lingonberries, that big Swedish furniture shop sells them… Everything but the pickles are freezable.

BATCH COOKABLE

LASTS FOR +3 DAYS
IN THE FRIDGE

GRIDDLED CHILLI PINEAPPLE, MIXED GREENS & MARIE ROSE

I am a huge Marie Rose fan, and also a big fan of a good sweet-and-sour combination. Eaten on its own or as part of a big feast this salad usually goes down a treat. It helps that it looks pretty too!

Serves 4

440 g (1 lb / 2¼ cups) quinoa
1 tablespoon olive oil

For the griddled pineapple
½ pineapple
1 tablespoon olive oil
sprinkle of red chilli flakes
  (red pepper flakes)
salt, to taste

For the Marie Rose
150 g (5 oz / ⅔ cup) Cashew
  Yoghurt (see page 140) or
  other plant yoghurt
2 tablespoons lemon juice
½ teaspoon sweet paprika
black pepper, to taste

To serve
2 baby gem lettuces
mixed greens and herbs
2 avocados, stoned and cut
  into quarters

Griddled pineapple

Chop the pineapple into slices and marinate with olive oil and sprinkles of chilli while you cook the quinoa.

Cook the quinoa following the packet instructions. Once cooked, set aside to cool. Once cool, add some olive oil to a medium pan and fry the quinoa until crispy.

Turn the heat to medium and dry out the grains, stirring to move them about the pan. Once all the moisture has evaporated, continue cooking the quinoa until it has turned a nutty brown and starts to 'pop' – this will take about 10 minutes. Stir every so often to stop the quinoa burning.

Griddle the pineapple in a really hot griddle pan (grill pan) until you get pretty charred marks and the slices are caramelised. Set aside until you are ready to put your salad together.

Marie Rose

Place all the Marie Rose ingredients in a blender and blitz until well combined and you have a beautiful smooth, plant-based mayo.

Put the salad together. Start with the toasted quinoa, then the baby gem, mixed greens, herbs and avocado. Top off with the griddled pineapple and dollop over the creamy Marie Rose.

BATCH COOKABLE

FREEZABLE

LASTS FOR +3 DAYS
IN THE FRIDGE

TOMATO, SPICY ROCKET, WATERMELON & COMPRESSED FETA SALAD

This is a killer summer combination of a salad. It makes my heart sing and brings my tastebuds a lot of happiness too.

Serves 6

For the salad base
2 baby gem lettuces
1 small purple endive or chicory
handful of diced watermelon
¼ red onion, sliced
1 avocado, sliced
1 cucumber, ribboned
handful of cherry tomatoes, halved
handful of watercress
handful or rocket (arugula)
handful of basil

To serve
Macadamia Ricotta (see page 144)
Big Batch Dressing (see page 152)

Either use the macadamia nut cheese straight away as a soft, ricotta-type cheese or make the compressed feta, which will take more effort and time, but it's worth it! To ferment, add ½ tablespoon salt to the cheese mix and put the cheese into a nut milk bag – you can buy one of these in a health food store or online.

Place the bag with the cheese in a sieve on top of a bowl and add a heavy weight on top – perhaps a full jam jar, or anything that will apply a bit of weight to get rid of the excess liquid. Put the cheese in the fridge for 24 hours to 'age'.

When you are ready to serve, add all the salad ingredients to a beautiful bowl (remember, you feast with your eyes first) and arrange attractively.

Finally, add the macadamia cheese either in dollops (the lazy version) or in chunks (the time-consuming, eager version), and serve with the dressing on the side. Either way, this salad will taste refreshing, zingy and herby.

Tip   The feta is freezable.

BATCH COOKABLE

+3 DAYS

LASTS FOR +3 DAYS
IN THE FRIDGE

NUT-FREE

MULTI-VEGETABLE PAELLA & AVO AIOLI

After living in Spain for the last 11 years, this is my veggie contribution to Spain's beloved national dish. It's a jam-packed delicious version that converts the weary.

Serves 4–6

For the topping
(200 g / 7 oz) green beans
  or asparagus
1 small sweet potato, sliced
½ red (bell) pepper, sliced
1 bunch of cherry tomatoes
  on the vine
olive oil, for cooking

For the paella
1 onion, chopped
1 teaspoon sweet paprika
½ teaspoon saffron
1 tomato, chopped
4 sundried tomatoes, chopped
250 g (9 oz / 1 cup) aborio rice
  or other risotto rice
150 g (5 oz / 1 cup) frozen peas
750 ml (25 fl oz / 3 cups) boiling
  water, slightly more if needed
pink Himalayan salt and black
  pepper, to taste

For the avo-aioli
2 avocados, peeled and stoned
1 garlic clove, peeled and
  finely grated
juice of 1 lemon
1 tablespoon parsley, chopped

To serve
lemon or lime wedges
chopped parsley and basil

Preheat the oven to 220°C (430°F/Gas 7).

Topping

Coat all the topping vegetables with oil, then scatter over a baking tray (baking sheet) lined with greaseproof paper (wax paper) and cook for 15 minutes in the oven. After 15 minutes, lower the oven temperature to 200°C (400°F/Gas 6) and cook for another 15–20 minutes until the vegetables are soft on the inside and crispy on the outside.

Paella

In the meantime, in a big, deep pan start frying the onion with a good amount of olive oil. Add all the spices along with the fresh and sundried tomatoes and give it a good stir for 5–10 minutes.

Add the rice and gently fry for 5 minutes until it is well coated with all the spices. Add the frozen peas and boiling water to the pan. Put the heat on medium to low, cover with a lid and cook for 20 minutes. If you see that the water evaporates quickly and the rice is still not cooked, just add a bit more water. Go steady.

Avo-aioli

To make the avo-aioli, add all the ingredients except for the parsley into a blender and blitz until you have a nice smooth, creamy texture.

Finally add the parsley and give it a good mix. Add more salt and pepper if needed.

After 20 minutes check on the paella. Make sure that the rice is cooked and there is no liquid left. Arrange the roasted veggies on top in a beautiful pattern. Serve straight from the pan with lime or lemon wedges, sprinkles of parsley and basil with dollops of avo-aioli.

Tip

This dish can definitely be pre-prepared and just heated in the oven before serving. It's a showstopper and an amazing dish to serve to friends on a weekend.

BATCH COOKABLE

FREEZABLE

LASTS FOR +3 DAYS
IN THE FRIDGE

NUT-FREE IF
PLANT YOGHURT IS
USED INSTEAD OF
CASHEW YOGHURT

MOUSSAKA & TZATZIKI

A dish that deserves the time that it takes to prepare, and for me a reminder of many holidays spent in Bulgaria. The smell of my grandmother's and aunties' kitchens and memories of myself sat at the kitchen table peering at the hustle and bustle around me in a family that loved to cook.

Serves 4

1 whole leek, chopped, greens and all
2 carrots, chopped
olive oil, for cooking
1 aubergine (eggplant), chopped
2 large baking potatoes, chopped
1 green (bell) pepper, deseeded and chopped
2 tomatoes, chopped
1 bay leaf
1 tablespoon thyme leaves
1 x 400 g (14 oz) tin of tomatoes
250 ml (8½ fl oz / 1 cup) vegetable stock
500 ml (1 lb 2 oz / 2 cups) Cashew Yoghurt (see page 140) or any plant yoghurt
2 tablespoons Gluten-free Flour Mix (see page 146)
pink Himalayan salt and black pepper, to taste

For the tzatziki
375 g (13 oz / 1½ cups) Cashew Yoghurt (see page 140) or any plant yoghurt
¼ cucumber, finely chopped
½ garlic clove, peeled and grated
1 tablespoon chopped dill
juice of ½ lemon

Preheat the oven to 200°C (400°F/Gas 6).

In a big pan on a medium heat, add the leek and carrots to some olive oil and cook until soft for about 5 minutes. Add the aubergine, potato, pepper, tomatoes, bay leaf and thyme and cook for another 10 minutes.

Add the tinned tomatoes and stock and cook on a medium heat with a lid on for another 10 minutes.

Once the vegetables have softened, pour the mixture into an ovenproof dish and bake in the oven for about 30 minutes.

Tzatziki

Add all the tzatziki ingredients to a bowl, give them a good stir, then set aside.

Now start to assemble the moussaka. Mix either cashew yoghurt or your choice of plant yoghurt with 2 tablespoons of gluten-free flour mix and salt and pepper to taste. If it's too thick add water to thin it out.

Take the vegetables out of the oven and pour over the topping mixture – make sure the whole surface is covered. Heat the grill, pop the moussaka underneath and cook for 10 minutes or until the top is nice and golden brown.

Once browned let the moussaka cool for 10 minutes before serving with the tzatziki and some crispy greens.

Tip

Perfect dish for batch cooking. Make one of these at the beginning of the week and enjoy for the next few days at home or as a takeaway. It's also very freezable!

BATCH COOKABLE

FREEZABLE

+3 DAYS

LASTS FOR +3 DAYS
IN THE FRIDGE

CURRY WITH ALL THE SIDES: MINTY RAITA & CRUNCHY COCONUT TOPPER

Serves 4–6

Curry is such a great dish because you can include many different types of veggies and spices, which all marry together. This recipe makes a pretty big batch of curry paste but it will last you for weeks stored in the fridge – you only need to add 1–2 tablespoons to veggies for a super-quick curry.

Curry paste

Start by making the curry paste by adding all of the ingredients to a blender and blitzing to a paste. Store in a glass container in the fridge. The longer this sits in the fridge, the more fragrant the paste.

Curry

Heat 4 tablespoons of the curry paste in a medium pan and cook the onion for 5 minutes until soft, then add the aubergine, carrot, sweet potato and courgette and give it a good mix. Add the coconut milk and turn the heat down to medium, cover and simmer for about 20 minutes.

Once the vegetables are semi-soft, it's time to add the, broccoli, asparagus and kale. Give everything a good mix and leave to cook for another 10 minutes with the lid off.

Crunchy topper

Meanwhile, make the crunchy topper. Add all the ingredients to a small pan and gently toast the seeds, peanuts and coconut until golden brown and crunchy, then set aside.

Raita

Add all the raita ingredients into a bowl and give it a good mix. Leave in the fridge to chill while the curry is cooking.

Once the vegetables in the curry are cooked, the last thing you do before serving is stir in half a bag of spinach. This is a great way of eating greens and gives the curry extra freshness.

Serve the curry with a dollop of raita, a sprinkle of crunchy topping, a lime wedge for freshness and extra herbs if desired.

Tip

I always think curry tastes best if made in advance so that all the flavours can develop. Every element of this dish can be made up and gently heated before serving. Curries are a great way of using up sad vegetables that you haven't got to during the week.

For the curry paste
3 shallots
10 garlic cloves, peeled
2 red chillies, or just 1 if you want less heat
1 thumb-sized piece of fresh root ginger, grated
50 g (2 oz) fresh turmeric root or 2 tablespoons turmeric powder
1 tablespoon maple syrup
1 teaspoon salt
250 ml (8½ fl oz / 1 cup) olive oil
juice of 1 lime

For the curry
1 onion, chopped
½ aubergine (eggplant), chopped
1 carrot, chopped
1 sweet potato, chopped
½ courgette (zucchini), chopped
400 ml (13 fl oz / 1½ cups) coconut milk
100 g (3½ oz) broccoli florets
100 g (3½ oz) asparagus
100 g (3½ oz) kale
½ bag spinach leaves

For the crunchy topper
35 g (1 oz / ¼ cup) black sesame seeds
30 g (1 oz / ¼ cup) peanuts
25 g (1 oz / ¼ cup) desiccated (shredded) coconut

For the raita
250 ml (8½ fl oz / 1 cup) Cashew Yoghurt (see page 140) or any plant yoghurt
2 tablespoons finely chopped red onion
100 g (3½ oz) cucumber, deseeded and finely chopped
handful of mint, finely chopped, plus a few leaves for decoration

To serve
lime wedges
chopped herbs
Chickpea Flatbread (see page 130)
rice of your choice (optional)

DIPS &

SIDES

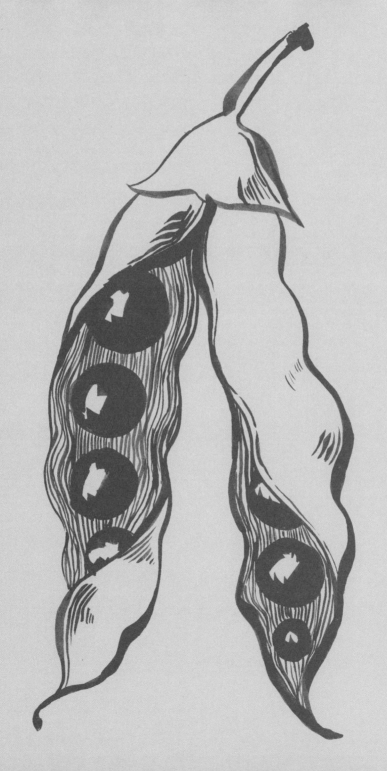

DIPS & SIDES

I love having options on the table, and these dips and sides are just that. They are add-ons to almost all of the recipes in this book that can be enjoyed together or as a side at a brunch or dinner, or if you have the time they can be batch cooked and kept in the fridge until needed. I have given away some family secrets in this chapter, but I am happy to share them with you!

BATCH COOKABLE

+3
DAYS

LASTS FOR +3 DAYS
IN THE FRIDGE

WICKED POTATO SALAD WITH DILL

You can't deny yourself a good potato – fact!
Especially if it is a potato salad that has the
added goodness of nuts, lentils and greens.
You simply can't go wrong.

Serves 4–6 as a sharing dish

85 g (3 oz / ½ cup) beluga lentils
600 g (1 lb 5 oz) baby potatoes

For the dressing
60 ml (2 fl oz / ¼ cup) olive oil
2 tablespoons apple cider vinegar
1 small shallot, finely diced
1 tablespoon chopped dill, plus extra
  to garnish
½ tablespoon strong mustard
  (I love a good Dijon)
½ tablespoon maple syrup
1 tablespoon chopped capers
1 green apple, cored and
  finely diced
pink Himalayan salt and black
  pepper, to taste

To serve
handful of watercress
handful of baby spinach
30 g (1 oz / ¼ cup) raw walnuts

Cook the lentils following the packet instructions. Drain and set aside.

Next boil the potatoes in a big saucepan with a pinch of salt. Drain and set aside.

Dressing In a bowl, combine all the dressing ingredients, giving everything a good stir so that all the ingredients are properly incorporated. Then add the potatoes and beluga lentils and give it a stir.

Add the watercress, baby spinach, extra dill and walnuts just before serving so that they don't get too soggy from the dressing. Serve immediately.

Tip I always find that this salad tastes so much better the day after it has been made because that way the ingredients have had time to marry. Just make sure you leave the leafy bits out until you are ready to serve.

BATCH COOKABLE

FREEZABLE

LASTS FOR +5 DAYS
IN THE FRIDGE

NUT-FREE

CREAMY COCONUT
RED LENTIL DAL

The trustworthy lentil – filling, easy to cook and a great addition to any meal. I love this dish as a side to the curry feast or as a dip with some home-made bread (on page 122), particularly the Chickpea Flatbread (see page 130) or with corn nachos.

Makes 4 portions for sharing

400 g (14 oz / 2 cups) red lentils
1 tablespoon olive oil
1 shallot
1 tablespoon tomato purée (paste)
1 teaspoon sumac
1 teaspoon sweet paprika
2 medjool dates, stoned (pitted) and torn
250 ml (8 fl oz / 1 cup) coconut milk
salt, to taste

To serve
lime wedge

Cook the red lentils following the packet instructions. Drain, then set aside.

Heat the olive oil in a large pan and fry the shallot until nice and soft and translucent. Add the tomato purée, sumac and sweet paprika and give it a good stir.

Add the lentils, dates and coconut milk and lower the heat to a gentle simmer.

Let the lentils simmer for 10–15 minutes until they have thickened and are a nice creamy texture with a little bit of bite. Serve straightaway or take off the heat and cover with a lid until ready to serve.

Tip

This is a great side dish to keep in the fridge and use as an add-on to any bowl, as a pâté on toast or just enjoyed as a stew with a cooked grain, such as quinoa or rice.

BATCH COOKABLE

FREEZABLE

LASTS FOR +5 DAYS
IN THE FRIDGE

NUT-FREE

MY GRAN'S BUTTER BEAN DIP WITH STICKY SWEET LEEKS

The topping of the butter bean dip is what makes this dish. It's sticky and sweet and utterly delightful. This dip has been a steady favourite on dinner-party tables and is a fridge staple because it's so versatile. It can also be used as a pâté or dolloped into almost any dish. (See picture overleaf.)

Makes 6 portions

For the dip
400 g (14 oz) dried butter beans (lima beans), or use tinned
60 ml (2 fl oz / ¼ cup) water
juice of ½ lemon
pink Himalayan salt and black pepper, to taste

For the topping
80 ml (2½ fl oz / ⅓ cup) olive oil
1 leek, finely chopped, greens and all
½ teaspoon chilli flakes (red pepper flakes)
1 tablespoon maple syrup
1 teaspoon sweet paprika

To serve
chopped parsley or coriander (cilantro)
chopped nuts and seeds

Dip	Cook the beans following the packet instructions or choose the easy route and use good-quality cooked butter beans from a tin.
	In a blender, blitz all the dip ingredients together until you have a fine, smooth, creamy dip. Spoon out into a semi-deep bowl or plate and give it a swirl over the base.
Topping	For the topping, heat the olive oil in a pan over a medium heat and cook the leek for about 10 minutes until it starts to soften. Add some salt to taste along with the chilli flakes, maple syrup and paprika and cook for another 5–10 minutes until you have a sticky, beautiful texture.
	Spread the topping evenly over the top of the dip and drizzle with the lovely scented oil that is left in the pan.
	This dip is fantastic as a side dish or as a starter dip with focaccia (see page 124). You can make this ahead of time, it lasts for up to a week in the fridge.
Tip	Make this one of your fridge staples. Lasts for a week, tastes good on anything and is a great alternative to hummus. Add the topping to the dip and freeze the together.

Chickpea Flatbread
& Marinated Crunchy
Chickpeas

Nan's Sweet
& Sour Pickles

Soljee's Kimchi

Courgettes in
Creamy Garlic
Sauce

My Gran's
Butter Bean
Dip with Sticky
Sweet Leeks

BATCH COOKABLE

FREEZABLE

LASTS FOR +2 DAYS

NUT-FREE

ROSEMARY & GARLIC FOCACCIA

Did someone say gluten-free focaccia? Oh yes, and it's really good, too. This bread goes with many of the recipes in this book. It's simple to make and the closest you will get to the real deal.

Makes 1 oven tray of bread, serves 4–6

1 tablespoon dry yeast or ½ cube of fresh yeast
1 teaspoon coconut sugar or maple syrup
2 tablespoons olive oil, plus extra for drizzling
375 g (13 oz / 3 cups) Gluten-free Flour Mix (see page 146)
pinch of pink Himalayan salt

For topping
rosemary and herbes de Provence mix

Preheat the oven to 200°C (400°F/Gas 6). Line a baking tray (baking sheet) with greaseproof paper (wax paper).

Add 370 ml (13 fl oz / 1½ cups) of water to a bowl and top up with 120 ml (4 fl oz / ½ cup) of boiling water.

Add the yeast along with a sprinkle of coconut sugar, maple syrup and give it a good mix. Add the olive oil and a pinch of salt and mix until the yeast is fully dissolved.

Gently fold in the flour and stir until everything is well incorporated. Don't worry if the mixture feels sticky, it's supposed to be. Leave the mixture somewhere warm, covered with a tea towel, for 30–40 minutes.

Drizzle a good amount of olive oil over the lined baking tray, then carefully spoon over the dough, wetting your fingers and spreading it out with your hands. Finally sprinkle some salt, rosemary and herbes de Provence over the top and stick the tray in the oven for 30 minutes. For the final 5 minutes, put the bread right at the top of the oven so that it takes on a lovely golden colour.

Once the bread is done, transfer to a wire rack to cool briefly, then serve immediately.

BATCH COOKABLE

+1
DAYS

LASTS FOR +1 DAYS

NUT-FREE

MAPLE-GLAZED SESAME KALE CRISPS

I have made these as pre-nibbles on many occasions. They are also great as a movie snack. Easy, tasty and quick!

Serves 1–2

1 bag of kale
1 tablespoon maple syrup
3 tablespoons olive oil
1 tablespoon sesame seeds

Preheat the oven to 200°C (400°F/Gas 6).

Start by taking the stems off the kale and discarding these, putting the leaves into a big bowl.

Add the maple syrup and olive oil to the bowl and massage the kale well, making sure that all the leaves are coated.

Line a baking tray (baking sheet) with greaseproof paper (wax paper) and spread the kale over it. Evenly sprinkle with sesame seeds and put the tray in the oven for 20 minutes. Make sure you check it halfway through to makes sure it does not burn.

The crisps should be golden and crispy when they are done, and must be eaten immediately.

SOLJEE'S KIMCHI

Korea has hundreds of versions of this dish. Kimchi is a fermented cabbage or vegetable that is traditionally flavoured with many ingredients. This is my simple plant-based version that has a kick. You can vary how much garlic, chilli and ginger add. I personally prefer my kimchi more gingery than garlicky. (See picture on page 121.)

Makes 1 x small or medium jar (depending on the size of your cabbage)

1 tablespoon salt
½ head green cabbage, thinly sliced
¼ head red cabbage, thinly sliced
1 carrot, finely chopped lengthwise
½ red (bell) pepper, finely chopped lengthways

For the flavouring paste
½ red (bell) pepper, deseeded and chopped
1 tablespoon minced ginger
½ tablespoon minced garlic
1 green spring onion (scallion)
1 red chilli
pinch of pink Himalayan salt

Massage the salt into the cabbage slices until they start releasing liquid. This liquid is what you will eventually be using as your brine to ferment the kimchi.

Flavouring paste In a blender or using a pestle and mortar, combine all the flavouring ingredients into a paste.

Check on your massaged cabbage and make sure you have released enough liquid. Gently massage the paste into the cabbage, chop finely, add the carrot and pepper and transfer to a clean, large glass jar with a lid.

Make sure you press the cabbage into the jar properly so that it is covered by the cabbage liquid. It is very important that all the veggies are covered with a sufficient amount of brine and pressed down properly.

Leave the jar to sit at room temperature for at least 2–3 days, opening up and 'burping' the kimchi at least once a day. After 2–3 days, the kimchi is ready to eat and can be refrigerated until needed. The fermentation will still continue in the fridge but at a much slower rate. Always use clean utensils when dipping into kimchi to avoid spoilage.

The longer the kimchi sits and ferments, the more flavourful it becomes.

BATCH COOKABLE

LASTS FOR +7 DAYS
IN THE FRIDGE

NUT-FREE

NAN'S SWEET & SOUR PICKLES

Having a Norwegian grandmother, who was also a very good cook, gave me a whole other repertoire of favourite dishes. These pickles go very well with any heavy or spicy foods. The acidity and slight sweetness create a party of flavours in your mouth. (See picture on page 120.)

Makes 1 x 500 g (1 lb 2 oz) jar

2 cucumbers (English)
1 tablespoon pink Himalayan salt
375 ml (13 fl oz / 1½ cups) water
120 ml (4 fl oz / ½ cup) apple
    cider vinegar
120 ml (4 fl oz / ½ cup) maple syrup
1 bay leaf
2 allspice berries
1 tablespoon finely chopped dill
1 tablespoon finely chopped
    red onion

Slice the cucumber thinly on a mandolin or use a cheese slicer. Put the slices in a bowl, toss them with the salt, and leave to stand for about 20 minutes.

Combine the water, vinegar, maple syrup, bay leaf and allspice in a medium pan and bring to a boil. Once boiling, immediately remove from the heat and leave to cool and infuse.

Rinse the salt off the cucumbers, drain and squeeze out as much moisture as possible. Put the cucumbers in a medium bowl and add the cooled pickling solution – they should be completely covered by the brine. Pour everything into a clean jar and refrigerate for at least 3–6 hours before serving.

You can make a bigger batch if you prefer, as the cucumbers will last for at least a few weeks in the fridge. Just make sure you always use a clean utensil when helping yourself to the pickles to avoid spoilage.

BATCH COOKABLE

FREEZABLE

LASTS FOR +5 DAYS
IN THE FRIDGE

NUT-FREE

SMOKY SUMAC GREEN BEANS

This recipe was handed down to me by two amazing Egyptian clients who insisted that they teach me one of their traditional dishes. I have been cooking this dish ever since and it is a retreat classic whenever I can source good-quality beans.

Serves 4

500 g (1 lb 2 oz) green beans –
   any type, flat or French, it's up
   to you, trimmed
olive oil, for frying
3–4 garlic cloves, peeled and sliced
1 yellow onion, sliced
1 teaspoon sumac
½ teaspoon chilli flakes
   (red pepper flakes)
400 g (14 oz) tin of good-quality
   tomatoes
1–2 medjool dates, stoned (pitted)
pink Himalayan salt and black
   pepper, to taste

To serve
fresh parsley or coriander (cilantro)
handful of watercress or rocket
   (arugula) and chopped nuts

Tidy up the beans – if you are using big flat beans, chop them into 4 pieces, if you are using French beans, cut them in half.

Heat a good glug of olive oil in a large pan. Add the garlic and onion and gently fry for about 10 minutes.

Add the sumac and chilli and give everything a good stir, then add the beans, salt and pepper and tomatoes, put a lid on and gently simmer for 15 minutes.

Check on the beans once and give them a stir. For the last 10 minutes of cooking, tear a date or 2 into the mix and stir. Take the lid off and let it simmer.

This can be eaten straightaway or made and enjoyed later, as long as it's stored in an airtight container. I like to top mine with rocket, chopped nuts and some parsley or coriander.

COURGETTES IN CREAMY GARLIC SAUCE

A plant-based version of a dish I have enjoyed many times during my summers spent in Bulgaria. Perfect alongside barbecues or as a cooling dip with a spicy dish.

Serves 4

olive oil, for frying
4 courgettes (zucchini), sliced
  about 5 mm (¼ in) thick,
  skin and all
½ garlic clove, peeled
1 tablespoon chopped dill
225 g (8 oz / 1 cup) Cashew
  Yoghurt (see page 140) or plain
  plant yoghurt
60 ml (2 fl oz / ¼ cup) water
  (to thin out the Cashew Yoghurt)
juice of ½ lemon, more if needed
pink Himalayan salt and black
  pepper, to taste

To serve
handful of greens, such as
  watercress or rocket (arugula)
sprigs of dill

Heat a good glug of olive oil in a frying pan (skillet) and fry the courgette slices, turning them once, until golden brown on each side. Once cooked, put them in a bowl. Repeat until all the slices are cooked. This part is a bit time-consuming but I promise it will be so worth it. I used to watch my grandmother do this all the time.

Once all the courgette is cooked, grate the garlic into the bowl, then add the dill and all the rest of the ingredients and give everything a gentle mix. You want to keep the courgettes as intact as possible.

Serve immediately or keep for later. Garnish with sprigs of dill and some greens, such as rocket or watercress.

BATCH COOKABLE

FREEZABLE

LASTS FOR +5 DAYS
IN THE FRIDGE

NUT-FREE

CHICKPEA FLATBREAD & MARINATED CRUNCHY CHICKPEAS

This is the result of creating a bread that contains it all: crunch, sweetness and spiciness all married together. It's a typical over-the-top dish that incorporates everything that I love, and it goes well with so many dishes in this book.

Makes 1 big oven tray, serves 4–6

For the flatbread
140 g (5 oz / 1 cup) chickpea (gram) flour
140 g (5 oz / 1 cup) Gluten-free Flour Mix (see page 146)
500 ml (17 fl oz / 2 cups) water
pinch of pink Himalayan salt
1 tablespoon bicarbonate of soda (baking soda)
black sesame seeds

For the caramelised onions
2–3 tablespoons olive oil
1 yellow onion, sliced
½ teaspoon sweet paprika
2–3 medjool dates, stoned (pitted) and torn or finely chopped

For the marinated chickpeas
400 g (14 oz) tin chickpeas, drained
½ teaspoon sesame seeds
½ teaspoon dried parsley
½ teaspoon red chilli flakes (red pepper flakes)
pinch of pink Himalayan salt

To serve
coriander (cilantro) and mint, chopped

Preheat the oven to 200°C (400°F/Gas 6) and line a baking tray (baking sheet) with greaseproof paper (wax paper).

Flatbread
In a bowl combine all the bread ingredients and set aside.

Caramelised onions
Next, start on the caramelised onions. Heat a good glug of olive oil in a pan and fry the onion for 10 minutes until nice and soft.

Add the sweet paprika along with the dates, give it a stir and set aside.

Marinated chickpeas
Drain the chickpeas very well – you can even pat them dry with a towel. Put them in a bowl and add the rest of the marinade ingredients, then stir to coat the chickpeas and set aside.

Drizzle a bit of olive oil over the lined baking tray and spoon the bread mixture over the tray. Make sure the mixture is spread out evenly with a spatula.

Sprinkle the chickpeas evenly over the top along with dollops of the caramelised onions. Make sure that every bite will have a little bit of both mixtures. Scatter over the sesame seeds.

Stick the tray in the middle of the oven and cook for 20 minutes. After the bread is done, move it to the top of the oven for 5 minutes or under the grill to give the chickpeas an extra crunch, but keep an eye on it to make sure they don't burn.

Take the bread out of the oven and transfer to a wire rack to cool. Serve immediately as a side dish or as a starter bread with any of the dips and sides in this chapter and sprinkled with chopped herbs.

FAVOURITE

BASICS

FAVOURITE BASICS

Welcome to the basics. These are starter recipes that will form the foundation of many of the other recipes in this book, and they are great to have ready prepped. You can taste the difference between shop-bought and home-made pesto or nut milks, and it's so much easier to reach for a ready-blended gluten-free flour mix rather than having to weigh everything out each time it is needed. It's worth setting aside a little time to prep these ahead – you can have a basics cooking day and make batches to store for another busy day.

BATCH COOKABLE

FREEZABLE

LASTS FOR 3-4 DAYS
IN THE FRIDGE

NUT-FREE

INSTANT HEMP MILK

This is one of the quickest milks you can make at home. It is my go-to milk when I am in a hurry and is particularly good in smoothies.

Serves 1

50 g (2 oz / ¼ cup) hemp hearts, hulled
500 ml (17 fl oz / 2 cups) water

Add-ins
½ vanilla pod (bean), scraped, or pinch of ground vanilla pod
stoned (pitted) dates, for sweetness
ground cinnamon, to taste
ground cardamom, to taste

Put the hemp hearts and water into a blender and blitz until you get a milky texture. Don't bother straining the milk, just use it straightaway. This is the quickest plant milk you will ever make!

Add-ins

You can add flavours by using any of the suggested add-ins. The milk lasts for 3–4 days in the fridge and is best stored in a glass bottle.

BATCH COOKABLE

FREEZABLE

LASTS FOR +4 DAYS
IN THE FRIDGE

PISTACHIO MILK

Pistachio milk is something that you still can't buy in supermarkets, therefore it is totally worth making this from scratch. Enjoyed cold or as a topping on porridge, it is hands down yummy. For all these nut milks, soaking the nuts before blending is an important step because it makes them easier to work with.

Makes 1 litre (34 fl oz)

110 g (3¾ oz / ¾ cup) pistachios
1 litre (34 fl oz / 4 cups) water
pinch of salt
½ vanilla pod (bean), scraped,
   or pinch of ground vanilla pod
1 teaspoon maple syrup
1 teaspoon rose water (optional)

Start by soaking the pistachios for 1 hour. All you need to do is put them in a bowl and just cover them with water. Once soaked, drain the nuts and tip them into a blender. Discard the soaking water and add the fresh water to the blender before blitzing until you have a lovely light green milk. Line a sieve with a muslin cloth, or use a nut milk bag or a fine strainer set over a bowl to separate the nut pulp from the milk. Pour in the milk and let it drain through.

Once you have your lovely milk, pour it back into the blender and add a pinch of salt, the vanilla and sweetener of choice, then blend everything together.

Pour the finished milk into a clean glass bottle and store in the fridge ready to use. It will last for up to 4 days.

Tip

You can use the leftover pulp from the milk to make little energy balls, or keep it in the fridge and add it to your smoothies, as it still contains lots of fibre.

ALMOND MILK

A classic milk and one that is so simple to make from scratch. Most of us find it more convenient to buy almond milk nowadays, but I promise, you will taste the difference when you try the home-made version.

Makes 1 litre (34 fl oz)

60 g (2 oz / ⅓ cup) raw almonds
1 litre (34 fl oz / 4 cups) water
pinch of salt

Add-ins
½ vanilla pod (bean), scraped,
  or pinch of ground vanilla pod
stoned (pitted) dates, for sweetness
ground cinnamon
ground cardamom
ground turmeric
ground cloves
orange or lemon zest

Start by soaking the almonds for at least 12 hours or overnight.

The water tends to get brown and mucky, so make sure you refresh it at least once. Once soaked, drain the nuts and tip them into a blender. Discard the soaking water, add the fresh water and blend until you have a lovely frothy milk.

Line a sieve with a muslin cloth (cheesecloth), or use a nut milk bag or a fine strainer set over a bowl to separate the nut pulp from the milk. Pour in the milk and let it drain through.

Pour the milk back into the blender, add a pinch of salt and blend again.

Pour the finished milk into a clean glass bottle and store in the fridge ready to use. It will last for up to 4 days.

Add-ins   Use any of the add-in alternatives. Even just a pinch of these will make your milk sing.

Tip   Some nuts are soaked to get rid of enzyme inhibitors; by soaking these specific nuts you make them easier to digest and the nutrients become more accessible.

BATCH COOKABLE

FREEZABLE

**LASTS FOR +7 DAYS
IN THE FRIDGE**

**CAN BE NUT-
FREE IF YOU USE
SUNFLOWER
SEEDS INSTEAD OF
CASHEWS**

CASHEW YOGHURT

This is one of the most important basics in this book, and the most versatile. The neutral taste of cashews makes this yoghurt ideal as a base in many of the recipes throughout the book. It is super easy to make, and lasts for a long time, too.

Makes 1 x 500 g (1 lb 2 oz) jar

280 g (10 oz / 1¾ cups) cashews
250 ml (8½ fl oz / 1 cup) water
½ probiotic capsule

Start by soaking the cashew nuts for 2 hours. All you need to do is add them into a bowl and cover with water. Drain the soaked nuts and tip them into a blender. Discard the soaking water, add the fresh water and the probiotic capsule into a blender and blitz until you get a smooth texture.

If you are doing this in a high-speed blender, make sure not to overheat the mixture as this will kill off the probiotics.

Once blended, transfer to a glass or plastic container. Do not use a metal one as the mixture won't ferment. Leave the container outside the fridge for 24 hours with a tea towel or muslin cloth on top so that the mixture can breathe, and to keep out any insects flies.

After 24 hours the mixture will be slightly fizzy and bubbly, which means it has fermented, so give it a good mix. Place a proper top on the glass container and leave it in the fridge for later use.

The yoghurt will last for up to 7 days in the fridge ready to use.

Tip

If you're in a hurry, soften the cashews by pouring hot water on them and soak them for 15 minutes. Make sure you cool them off in cold water before blending. I would recommend soaking them for 2 hours, but I understand that we are all busy bees!

If you are allergic to nuts, the cashews can be substituted with sunflower seeds. Just follow the same measurements and method.

BATCH COOKABLE

FREEZABLE

LASTS FOR +5 DAYS
IN THE FRIDGE

CAN BE NUT-
FREE IF YOU USE
SUNFLOWER
SEEDS INSTEAD OF
CASHEWS

CASHEW CHEESE

This is the same method and ingredients as the cashew yoghurt but is used as a cheese base. The difference? This version is thicker and lends itself well to making cashew cheese.

Makes 1 x 500 g (1 lb 2 oz) jar

280 g (10 oz / 1¾ cups) cashews
125 ml (4 fl oz / ½ cup) water
½ probiotic capsule

Exactly the same method for making the yoghurt but with less water. The mixture will become thicker and lend itself more easily into making a cheese.

BATCH COOKABLE

FREEZABLE

LASTS FOR MORE
THAN +7 DAYS IN OR
OUT OF THE FRIDGE

ALMOND BUTTER

This is a fantastic store-cupboard essential and is used throughout this book. It is easy and cheap to make, lasts a long time and tastes better than anything you will buy in a store.

Makes 1 x 500 g (1 lb) jar

240 g (8½ oz / 1½ cups) raw almonds
160 ml (5 fl oz / ⅔ cup) melted
   coconut butter
½ teaspoon ground cinnamon
½ teaspoon ground cardamom
pinch of grated nutmeg
pinch of salt
1 whole vanilla pod (bean), roughly
   chopped (I like to use all of it in
   a nut butter so nothing goes
   to waste)

Place the almonds in a food processor and blitz until you get a fine powder, then continue for about another 5 minutes.

Add the rest of the ingredients and blend until you have a lovely smooth butter.

Store in a clean glass jar outside the fridge. If you decide to keep it in the fridge, bear in mind that it will solidify.

BATCH COOKABLE

FREEZABLE

**LASTS FOR +7 DAYS
IN THE FRIDGE**

**CAN BE NUT-
FREE IF YOU USE
SUNFLOWER
SEEDS INSTEAD OF
CASHEWS**

COCONUT YOGHURT

Coconut yoghurt is something that we now can get in most supermarkets. While making it from scratch is a tad time-consuming, it is so worth it for the much-improved flavour.

Makes 1 x 500 g (1 lb 2 oz) jar

150 g (5 oz / 1 cup) cashews
250 ml (8½ fl oz / 1 cup)
   coconut water
meat of 1 young green coconut
   (buy ready to use or open a
   coconut and scrape it out yourself)
½ probiotic capsule

Start by soaking the cashew nuts for 2 hours; just put them in a bowl and cover with water.
Open up the coconut with a coconut opener or with a cleaver at a 90-degree angle.
Be careful if you have not done this before.

Drain and reserve the water, then scrape out the coconut meat, cutting off any brown parts that come away from the bottom of the coconut.

Drain the cashews and tip them into a blender with the coconut meat, coconut water and probiotic, then blitz until you get a smooth texture.

If you are doing this in a high-speed blender, make sure you don't overheat the mixture as this will kill off the probiotics.

Once blended, transfer to a glass or plastic container. Do not use a metal container as the mixture won't ferment. Leave outside the fridge for 24 hours with a tea towel or muslin cloth (cheesecloth) on top so that the mixture can breathe.

After 24 hours your mixture will be slightly fizzy and bubbly, which means it has fermented. Give it a good mix, put a top a on the glass container and leave in the fridge for later use. It will last for up to 7 days in the fridge.

Pimp your yoghurt with lemon zest, vanilla, orange zest or sweetener of choice. I personally love a squeeze of maple syrup and a drop of vanilla extract.

Tip

If you would like a quick coconut yoghurt, skip the probiotic and fermentation step and use the mixture straight after blending it into a silky smooth texture.

BATCH COOKABLE

FREEZABLE

**LASTS FOR +7 DAYS
IN THE FRIDGE**

MACADAMIA RICOTTA

Creamy, indulgent and the closest you are ever going to get taste-wise to a ricotta cheese. Once made it lasts for a good week. It is really versatile because there are endless flavour options and it can be used in many different recipes throughout this book.

Makes 1 x 500 g (1 lb 2 oz) jar

280 g (10 oz / 2 cups)
  macadamia nuts
160 ml (5 fl oz / ⅔ cup) water
½ probiotic capsule
pinch of salt

Start by soaking the macadamia nuts for 2 hours by putting them in a bowl and covering with water.

Drain the nuts and tip them into a blender along with the water and probiotic and blitz until you get a smooth texture. As this is a ricotta-style cheese the texture can be slightly bitty, which I personally love. If you are doing this in a high-speed blender, make sure not to overheat the mixture as this will kill off the probiotics.

Once blended, transfer to a clean glass or plastic container. Do not use a metal one as the mixture won't ferment. Leave the container outside the fridge for 24 hours with a tea towel or muslin cloth (cheesecloth) on top so that the mixture can breathe.

After 24 hours your mixture will be slightly fizzy and bubbly. Place a proper top on and leave in the fridge until you need it. It will last for up to 7 days in the fridge.

Tip

This is a great fridge basic. Dairy is the hardest food group to replace both taste-wise and on a comfort level. Many of my clients suffer from dairy intolerances and this has been a lifesaver in terms of being able to add some comfort back into your diet.

BATCH COOKABLE

FREEZABLE

LASTS FOR +14 DAYS IN THE FRIDGE

NUT PARMESAN

Being married to a partially Italian man with an Italian father, I knew I had to figure out a way of including a 'Parmesan-like' topping on some of my dishes. This works really well with pasta dishes, salads, soups and bowl foods.

Makes 1 x 150 g (5 oz) jar

60 g (2 oz / ½ cup) almond flour
60 g (2 oz / ½ cup) unsalted
  hazelnuts, or buy toasted
  if you prefer
1 tablespoon salt

Add-ins
chilli flakes (red pepper flakes) –
  for the daring spice lovers
1 teaspoon nutritional yeast –
  for the fully fledged vegans

If you don't have pre-toasted hazelnuts, start by toasting the nuts in a hot frying pan (skillet) until slightly brown and let cool.

Once cool, either crush in a pestle and mortar or whizz in a food processor or coffee grinder until you get a chunky consistency.

Simply mix the rest of the ingredients together and you have the perfect sprinkle for pasta dishes, salads and anything you would normally grate Parmesan over.

Add-ins

Use either of the add-ins for extra flavour impact

Store in an airtight glass jar in the fridge, where it will keep for 2 weeks.

Tip

Add 1 tablespoon of nutritional yeast into the mix. It has a cheesy, slightly acidic flavour and will enhance the overall taste, but is not necessary if you can't get hold of it.

BATCH COOKABLE

FREEZABLE

LASTS FOR +5 DAYS
IN THE FRIDGE

NUT-FREE

VANILLA CUSTARD

I grew up loving custard, it was one of my staple foods as a child. This lovely recipe is a great alternative and a fantastic base for several sweet treats.

Makes 500 ml (17 fl oz / 2 cups), serves 4

2 tablespoons very fine cornflour (cornstarch), such as Maizena
500 ml (17 fl oz / 2 cups) coconut milk (preferably from a Tetra Pak that is consistently creamy and doesn't separate)
3 tablespoons maple syrup
1 whole vanilla pod (bean), scraped

Blend the cornflour with a little bit of of the coconut milk in a medium pan over a medium heat, whisking until you have an even consistency. Then add the rest of the ingredients including the scraped vanilla pod – there is still a lot of goodness there – whisking until the cornflour and vanilla are fully incorporated into the coconut milk.

Whisk until the custard starts to thicken and then, as soon as the mixture begins to boil, take it off the heat and let it cool.

BATCH COOKABLE

FREEZABLE

LASTS FOR +3 DAYS
IN THE FRIDGE

NUT-FREE

GLUTEN-FREE FLOUR MIX

Many shop-bought gluten-free flour mixes can be unpredictable. Make a double batch of this and you will thank me later. It is not only practical but, more importantly, it works a treat!

Makes 900 g (2 lb) flour

210 g (7½ oz / 1⅓ cups) brown rice flour
140 g (5 oz / 1 cup) buckwheat flour
70 g (2½ oz / ½ cup) white rice flour
40 g (1½ oz / ½ cup) oat flour
40 g (1½ oz / ¼ cup) potato starch/flour
40 g (1½ oz / ½ cup) tapioca flour

Mix all the flours together and store in an airtight container.

BATCH COOKABLE

FREEZABLE

+3 DAYS

LASTS FOR +3 DAYS IN THE FRIDGE

NUT- AND YEAST-FREE

SUPER BREAD

My love of bread has always been immense. Discovering my gluten intolerance was not a very good day, to say the least. Faced with many shop-bought options I decided to make my own version of hearty bread. Inspired by the traditional Irish soda bread I thought I'd make this version yeast free too. Double whammy.

Makes 1 loaf

280 g (10 oz / 2 cups) Gluten-free Flour Mix (see page 146)
40 g (1½ oz / ¼ cup) ground flaxseeds
1 teaspoon bicarbonate of soda (baking soda)
pinch of salt
½ red or green apple, sliced
625 ml (2½ fl oz / 2½ cups) water

Add-ins
pumpkin seeds
sesame seeds
sunflower seeds
poppy seeds

Preheat the oven to 170°C (340°F/Gas 3).

Put all the dry ingredients into a bowl.

Put the apple into a blender with the water and blitz until fully incorporated.

Mix the apple water with the dry ingredients until you have a porridge-like consistency. The salt, bicarbonate of soda and the sweetness from the apple will all activate each other and make the bread lighter and fluffier.

Pour the mixture into a 450 g (1 lb) bread tin or good-quality silicone mould – the latter is my favourite. Top with seeds, if you like, and bake in the oven for 45–60 minutes until golden brown. Check after 45 minutes – insert a wooden skewer in the centre to see if it comes out dry. If it does, switch the oven off and let the bread set for another 15 minutes in the oven.

Once ready, transfer to a wire rack and leave to cool. The bread will last up to a week in the fridge and can easily be sliced and frozen. Great to just pop into the toaster when needed.

Tip

Refrigerate after one day. It will firm up the bread more, will be easier to slice and will last longer. This bread also lends itself well to freezing. Make sure you slice it first, though.

BATCH COOKABLE

FREEZABLE

+7 DAYS

LASTS FOR +7 DAYS
IN THE FRIDGE

NUT-FREE

PUMPKIN SEED PESTO

Pesto is one of my favourite fridge staples –
it lasts forever, tastes good on anything and
is super easy to make. This particular recipe is
made with pumpkin seeds and was developed
for clients with nut allergies. Personally,
I think pumpkin seeds have a great depth of
flavour and bring some fantastic nutritional
value to the table. It has even been approved
by my full-blooded Italian father in-law.

Makes 1 x 250 g (9 oz) jar

250 ml (8½ fl oz / 1 cup) olive oil,
  plus extra for sealing
120 g (4 oz / 1 cup) pumpkin seeds
bunch of basil (30 g / 1 oz)
1 garlic clove, peeled
½ tablespoon each salt
  and black pepper

Simply add all the ingredients to a blender and blitz until you have a lovely pesto.
You can choose to blend until smooth or to a chunkier consistency, if you prefer.

Tip

The fantastic thing about this recipe is that it will keep in the fridge for at least 2 weeks.
When you put it into a clean storage jar, make sure you cover the top of the mixture with
a good layer of oil, as it serves as a natural preservative. One centimetre (½ in) above the
pesto is more than enough.

BIG BATCH DRESSING

BATCH COOKABLE

FREEZABLE

+7 DAYS

LASTS FOR +7 DAYS
IN THE FRIDGE

NUT-FREE

Vegetables in general can be pretty boring, but I can tell you that a good dressing works wonders. And a tangy, tasty dressing that is available in your fridge at any given time is even better. This is a fantastic base that can be pimped up with different add-ins once one version becomes boring.

Makes 1 x 500 g (1 lb 2 oz) jar

250 ml (8 fl oz / 1 cup) olive oil
80 ml (2½ fl oz / ⅓ cup) apple
  cider vinegar
½ tablespoon salt
1 tablespoon Dijon mustard
1 tablespoon maple syrup
pepper, to taste

Add-ins
dill
shallots
red onion
sesame seeds
chives

Get a small glass jar, add all the ingredients and give it a good shake. This dressing will last for up to a week in the fridge and you can pimp it up with alternative add-ins when you want to perk up the basic flavour!

Tip

I love using recycled jars for this kind of thing. The perfect fridge staple – trust me!

BATCH COOKABLE

FREEZABLE

LASTS FOR +5 DAYS
IN THE FRIDGE

NUT-FREE

THE BEST NON-MEATBALLZ EVER

I have found the solution to missing meatballs! Inspired by my love of Swedish meatballs, this was the closest to those that I could get. They have depth of flavour, crunch and texture and are simple to make. These non-meatballz rock – I hope you love them as much as I do! (See pictures on pages 75 and 101.)

Makes 8 big balls or 14 small ones

75 g (2½ oz / ⅓ cup) brown rice
2–3 tablespoons olive oil
1 onion, finely diced
a sprig of thyme
6 tablespoons tamari
  soy sauce – more if you like
  your meatballs saltier
1 tablespoon Dijon mustard
240 g (8½ oz) black beans from
  a tin or jar (good-quality
  shop-bought), drained
60 g (2 oz / ⅔ cup) oat bran
3–4 tablespoons grapeseed oil
  or olive oil

Start by cooking the rice following the packet instructions.

In a medium pan, heat the olive oil and cook the onion, thyme, 3 tablespoons of tamari soy and the mustard. Cook for 5 minutes until the onion is nice and tender. Once cooked, take off the heat and set aside.

In a food processor, add the onion mix along with black beans and pulse. Don't overmix but blend until you have a sticky consistency.

Empty into a bowl and add the oat bran, cooked rice and remaining 3 tablespoons of tamari soy and give it a good mix.

Line a baking tray (baking sheet) with greaseproof paper (wax paper) and with a small or big ice-cream scoop, scoop out balls of mixture and gently roll until you have a round shape. Place them on to the paper until you are ready to cook them.

Heat the oil in a medium pan and cook the balls until they have a lovely crispy outside but are still nice and soft on the inside (5–10 minutes on each side should be enough).

The meatballz go really well with so many of the dishes in this book. As a side or part of a bowl meal, on a sandwich or with pasta, the options are endless!

Tip

These can be pre-rolled and stored in fridge until you want to cook them. These can also be baked in the oven. Preheat oven to 200°C (400°F/Gas 6) and bake for 20–30 minutes until you have a lovely crisp outside. If you are coeliac, make sure the oats are gluten free.

SWEET

TREATS

SWEET TREATS

Combining the five tastes – salt, savoury, sour, spicy and sweet – is an important element of eating and has been mentioned in various cultures that have trickled down their knowledge to us through hundreds of years. It is important that we adhere to this craving of ours, so this is a collection of my all-time favourite sweets to cook that have been inspired by my childhood, my adventures to numerous countries, clients and, last but not least, family favourites. Food is here to be enjoyed fully. Sweets and all!

BATCH COOKABLE

FREEZABLE

LASTS FOR +7 DAYS
IN THE FRIDGE

HAZELNUT BITES

Chocolate makes the heart sing, it makes you happy – there is no arguing about that! Make sure you make a big batch of these because they won't last long. They are the perfect holiday dessert, or actually, any occasion will do.

Makes 10 small bites

80 g (3 oz / ½ cup) hazelnuts, plus
  10 whole hazelnuts for the middle
80 g (3 oz / ¾ cup) almond flour
3 tablespoons cacao powder
60 ml (2 fl oz / ¼ cup) coconut oil
2 tablespoons peanut butter
3 medjool dates, stoned (pitted)

For the coating
200 g (7 oz) dark chocolate bar,
  90% or 70% cocoa solids

For the toppings
chopped hazelnuts
dried flower petals
  (for special occasions)

Place the hazelnuts in a small blender and blitz until you get a flour-like consistency. Then pulse until the mix becomes slightly sticky. Add in the rest of the ingredients and blitz until you get a sticky, fine mixture.

Spoon out bite-sized portions of mixture, place one whole hazelnut in the middle and wrap around it to form a ball, then place on a plate lined with greaseproof paper (wax paper). Do this until you have around 10 bite-sized balls, then place them in the fridge to set for 10–15 minutes.

In the meantime, break the chocolate into a bain marie – place a heatproof bowl over a saucepan with some boiling water in the bottom, but without the bowl touching the water, then cook, stirring occasionally, until it has melted. Remove the bowl from the pan.

Coating
& toppings

Line a chopping board or plate with greaseproof paper (wax paper), get the balls out of the fridge and gently dip and roll them in the melted chocolate until fully covered. Place the chocolate-covered balls on the paper and top with chopped hazelnuts and some dried flower petals. Place in the fridge to set.

These little tasty gems last for up to a week in the fridge but tend to be eaten pretty quickly!

BATCH COOKABLE

FREEZABLE

+5
DAYS

LASTS FOR +5 DAYS
IN THE FRIDGE

CHOCOLATE
CHIP COOKIES

Warning! Once you make these you won't
be able to stop eating them. They are great
to have around when you are feeling peckish
and need an energy boost. Or to have as
a takeaway.

Makes 8 big ones or 14 small ones

280 g (10 oz / 2 cups) raw
   whole cashews
160 g (5½ oz / 1 cup) almond flour
125 ml (4 fl oz / ½ cup) coconut oil

For the salted date caramel
8 medjool dates, stoned (pitted)
   and soaked in water for 1 hour,
   plus 4 tablespoons soaking liquid
1 tablespoon almond
   or peanut butter
½ vanilla pod (bean), finely chopped
a pinch of salt

Add-ins
100 g (3½ oz) chopped
   dark chocolate

Preheat the oven to 180°C (350°F/Gas 4). In a blender, add the cashews and blitz them until
they turn into a fine flour. Make sure to not overblend. Add the almond flour and coconut oil
and give it another whizz. Tip out the mixture into a bowl.

Salted date
caramel

Add all the caramel ingredients to a clean blender and blitz until you get a smooth caramel-like
consistency, then set aside. Spoon the salted caramel mixture into the bowl with the nut flours
along with the chopped chocolate. Slowly give it a mix with a big spoon – don't overmix as you
want to get mouthfuls of the chocolate and salted date caramel surprises.

Line a baking tray (baking sheet) with greaseproof paper (wax paper). Take a scoop of
cookie dough (use a proper ice-cream scoop – big or small, depending on the size you want
your cookies to be) and evenly scoop out balls onto the tray, there's no need to flatten them.

Cook in the oven for 10–15 minutes until the cookies have turned slightly golden brown.
Take out of the oven and let them cool completely on a wire rack. Once cooled, store the
cookies in an airtight container in the fridge for up to a week.

BATCH COOKABLE

FREEZABLE

+5
DAYS

LASTS FOR +5 DAYS
IN THE FRIDGE

STRAWBERRY & CREAM CAKE

Strawberries are one of my favourite berries, and make a very nice combination with coconut and sprigs of thyme. I love this cake and hope you do too.

Cuts into 10 slices

For the base
135 g (4½ oz / 1½ cups) desiccated
   (shredded) coconut
125 g (4 oz / 1¼ cup) almond flour
60 ml (2 fl oz / ¼ cup) coconut oil
pinch of salt

For the filling
500 g (1 lb 2 oz) strawberries
1 vanilla pod (bean), chopped
70 g (3 oz / ½ cup) cashews, soaked
   for at least 2 hours in cold water,
   or in hot water for 15 minutes
60 ml (2 fl oz / ¼ cup) coconut oil

For the topping
100 g (3 ½ oz) strawberries, halved
3 sprigs of thyme

To serve
strawberries
mint leaves

Base   Start by making the base for the cake by adding all the base ingredients to a blender and blitzing until you get a slightly sticky consistency. Line a 900g (2 lb) loaf tin with cling film (plastic wrap), so that the cake can easily be removed from the tin. Add the mixture and gently press down to get an even layer, just as you would with a traditional cheesecake base.

Filling   Place all the filling ingredients into a high-speed blender and blitz until everything is fully incorporated and you have a beautiful pink, even colour.

Topping   Pour the mixture into the tin and scatter the halved strawberries evenly along the filling and dot with sprigs of thyme. Place in the fridge for 2–3 hours to set.

Take the cake out of the fridge 30 minutes before you want to serve it to soften it up. Serve with fresh strawberries and a few mint leaves.

Tip   This cake can be made well in advance and is the perfect summer cooler.

CHOCOLATE GANACHE TORTE

Easy on the eye, this is the perfect companion to a dinner party and is bound to impress. If you want your friends to think you have put maximum effort into making a cake, this little number is your best shot!

Serves 6

For the base
240 g (8½ oz / 1¼ cups) hazelnuts
2 tablespoons cacao powder
6 medjool dates, stoned (pitted)
  and soaked for 1 hour
1 tablespoon coconut oil
pinch of salt

For the filling
250 ml (8½ fl oz / 1 cup) coconut oil
120 g (4 oz / 1 cup) cacao powder
60 ml (2 fl oz / ¼ cup) maple syrup

For the toppings
pinch of sea salt flakes
zest of 1 orange or ½ grapefruit

To serve
berries and fruits

Line a round 20 cm (8 ins) cake tin (pan) with a removable base with cling film (plastic wrap) for easy removal of the cake.

Base

For the base, place all the ingredients in a blender or food processor and blitz until you get a sticky consistency.

Pour the mixture into the lined tin, pressing it into the bottom in an even layer. Make the edge by pushing your thumb on the inside of the casing and shaping with your other thumb from the top, working your way all around. Then place in the fridge to chill and set for 10 minutes.

Filling

In a small saucepan over medium heat, gently heat all the filling ingredients. Do not overheat. If your coconut oil is solid, wait until it has melted before mixing until you have a shiny, beautiful mixture. Take off the heat. If your coconut oil is already melted you just need to incorporate all the ingredients and be very careful not to overheat.

Toppings

Pour the mixture into your beautiful tart crust. Evenly sprinkle some sea salt and some orange or grapefruit zest on top, then return to the fridge to set for 3 hours or until completely solidified.

Tip

This little number can be done way ahead of time. It will impress any dinner party-goer and can be topped off with berries and fruits for tartness.

CHERRY ALMOND CAKE

This cake just reminds me of comfort and warmth in one spoonful. I know I have been saying it a lot, but it is truly one of my favourites in this book. It's well worth the effort of pitting all of those cherries!

Cuts into 6 slices

140 g (5 oz / 1 cup) Gluten-free Flour Mix (see page 146)
200 g (7 oz / 1 cup) almond flour
250 ml (8 fl oz / 2 cups) Almond Milk or plant milk, shop-bought or home-made (see pages 137–139)
125 ml (4 fl oz / ½ cup) maple syrup
125 ml (4 fl oz / ½ cup) melted coconut oil
1 teaspoon baking powder
½ teaspoon bicarbonate of soda (baking soda)
small pinch of pink Himalayan salt
1 vanilla pod (bean), scraped
300 g (10½ oz) cherries, halved and pitted, saving a few whole ones to serve

To serve
Vanilla Custard (see page 146)

Preheat the oven to 180°C (350°F/Gas 4).

Line a 20 cm (8 ins) cake tin (pan) with greaseproof paper (wax paper) or use a good-quality silicone mould.

Add all the ingredients apart from the cherries to a food processor and blend everything together for about 5 minutes until well incorporated.

Pour the mixture into the cake tin (pan), then carefully arrange the cherries on top, making sure that every bite will have a cherry in it.

Bake in the middle of the oven for 35 minutes. For the last 5 minutes, place the cake under a preheated grill to give the cake a golden-brown finish.

Remove from the oven, then transfer to a wire rack to cool. I love this cake with a good helping of my special vanilla custard. Add fresh cherries on top.

STICKY TOFFEE PUDDING WITH STICKY TOFFEE SAUCE

It upset me for a very long time when I discovered that I was intolerant to gluten, particularly when I realised that I would not be able to enjoy one of my favourite desserts. I promise you this is better than the original.

Serves 6

250 ml (8½ fl oz / 1 cup) Almond Milk or plant milk, shop-bought or home-made (see pages 137–139)
300 g (10½ oz / 2 cups) medjool dates, stoned (pitted)
80 g (3 oz / ½ cup) coconut sugar
125 ml (4 fl oz / ½ cup) coconut oil
1 teaspoon bicarbonate of soda (baking soda)
95 g (3½ oz / ¾ cup) Gluten-free Flour Mix (see page 146)
1 vanilla pod (bean), seeds scraped
1 teaspoon ground cinnamon
½ teaspoon ground cardamom
½ teaspoon ground clove
pinch of pink Himalayan salt

For the sticky toffee sauce
140 g (5 oz / 1 cup) coconut sugar
250 ml (8½ fl oz / 1 cup) coconut milk
½ teaspoon salt

To serve
Vanilla Custard (see page 146)

Preheat the oven to 190°C (375°F/Gas 5). Line a 20 cm (8 ins) square cake tin (pan) with greaseproof paper (wax paper) or use a good-quality silicone mould.

Start with the pudding. In a small saucepan gently heat the milk and dates for 5–10 minutes until the dates have softened. Once softened, set aside.

In a blender, blitz the coconut sugar and coconut oil until the sugar has mostly disintegrated.

Add the bicarbonate of soda to the milk and date mix – it will start to fizz and bubble, but that is okay.

In a bowl, combine the flour, vanilla, spices, pinch of salt, coconut oil and sugar mix along with the dates and milk mixture and give everything a good stir.

Pour into the cake tin (pan) and bake in the oven for 30 minutes.

Sticky toffee sauce

While the pudding is cooking, make the sauce. Heat a pan over medium heat, add the coconut sugar and coconut milk and let it heat through.

Add the salt and bring to a boil, then reduce to a simmer and let it simmer for 20 minutes until the caramel has thickened. Stir it occasionally to make sure it doesn't burn. A great way of knowing if it's ready is to see if it sticks to the back of your spoon.

Stir in a little more salt if desired and either use it straightaway or let it cool down before storing in a glass jar – it will become even thicker as it cools.

Once the cake is done, transfer to a wire rack to cool and enjoy with a home-made custard and a drizzle of sticky toffee sauce.

Tip

The cake, custard and toffee sauce all last for a long time in the fridge – well, that is, if you can keep your hands off them! – or freezer.

BATCH COOKABLE

FREEZABLE

LASTS FOR +7 DAYS
IN THE FRIDGE

CHEWY CHOCOLATE BARS

Chewy, gooey and absolutely yummy.
These little bad boys are well worth making.
Don't blame me if you eat them all in one go!

Makes 6–10, depending on size

For the caramel layer
360 g (12 oz / 2¼ cups) medjool
   dates, stoned (pitted)
½ teaspoon coarse sea salt
1 vanilla pod (bean), scraped, or
   1 teaspoon ground vanilla pod
1 tablespoon nut butter (almond
   or peanut)

For the chewy base
80 g (3 oz / 1 cup) desiccated
   (shredded) coconut
140 g (5 oz / 1 cup) hazelnuts
2 dates, stoned (pitted)
3 tablespoons coconut oil
1 tablespoon cacao powder
small pinch of pink Himalayan salt
1 vanilla pod (bean), scraped, or
   1 teaspoon ground vanilla pod

For the chocolate layer
125 ml (4 fl oz / ½ cup) coconut oil
4 tablespoons cacao powder
3 tablespoons maple syrup

Caramel layer

Start by soaking the dates in water for at least 1 hour – use enough water to cover them. This is so that they are easier to blend.

Chewy base

In the meantime, make the chewy base by adding all the ingredients to a blender and blitzing until everything is combined and you have a semi-sticky mixture.

Place the mixture in a 450 g (1 lb) loaf tin or silicone mould. I like to line the tray with cling film (plastic wrap) so that it's easier to pop out when ready. Press down the mixture to create an even layer.

Next, whizz the dates with 50 ml (2 fl oz / ¼ cup) of the soaking liquid, the salt, vanilla and nut butter in a blender until you get a rich, silky smooth consistency. Evenly spread the caramel over the chewy base layer in the mould and let it set in the freezer for 2 hours.

Chocolate layer

When the mixture is almost set, start prepping the chocolate layer by melting the coconut oil on low heat. Once it starts melting, add the cacao powder and maple syrup and mix well together, then take off the heat.

Take the tin out of the freezer, pop out the mix and slice into 10 thin bars or 6 bigger bars.

Place a piece of baking parchment (parchment paper) on the work surface, then grab a fork and use it to pick up a bar and dip it in the chocolate mixture to coat. Sometimes it helps to have a spoon handy to spoon the chocolate over. Pop it straight on the paper – because the bars are semi frozen the chocolate will set straight away. Repeat with all the bars.

Place in the fridge and take out when ready to eat.

Tip

I often sprinkle chopped nuts on the top, but that's totally optional. These can be made in a big batch and kept in the freezer, although I warn you – they will disappear pretty quickly.

BATCH COOKABLE

FREEZABLE

+5 DAYS

LASTS FOR +5 DAYS
IN THE FRIDGE

EASY PEASY
CHOCOLATE MOUSSE

My daughter's favourite chocolate mousse.
A lovely alternative to dairy that I developed
for my clients with intolerances. It is tasty
and light and hopefully fills that chocolate
craving that we all get. This is also a great way
of not wasting chickpea water!

Makes 2 big glasses or 4 small pots

80 g (3 oz / ½ cup) cashews
150 ml (5 fl oz / ½ cup + 2 tablespoons)
    chickpea water or aquafaba (the
    liquid you get in the tin/Tetra Pak)
80 ml (3 fl oz / ⅓ cup) maple syrup
3 tablespoons cacao powder
1 vanilla pod (bean), scraped

To serve
fresh berries or currants
mint leaves

Soak the cashews for at least 2 hours or quick-soak them in boiling water for 20 minutes.

In a bowl, whisk the chickpea water until it becomes white and fluffy, just like beaten egg whites. Set aside or in the fridge.

Drain the nuts and add the soaked cashews, maple syrup, cacao powder, vanilla seeds and 2 tablespoons of water to a blender and blitz until you have a smooth texture.

Now, gently fold the chocolate mixture into the white fluffy chickpea mix with a spoon until it's well combined.

Ladle into serving glasses and let it set in the fridge for 1 hour.

Serve with fresh berries or currants and mint leaves.

Tip

This can be prepared in advance. For ease, always make sure you have a store of pre-soaked and drained cashews in the fridge in a glass container – they last for 3 days.

BATCH COOKABLE

FREEZABLE

+5 DAYS

LASTS FOR +5 DAYS
IN THE FRIDGE

NUT-FREE

THE EASIEST MANGO
VANILLA MOUSSE

I first made this dish in Zanzibar when
I had access to very good juicy mangoes
and home-made coconut oil. Now I get
to share the goodness with all of you.
(See picture opposite.)

Serves 4–6

600 g (1 lb 5 oz) chopped mature
    sweet mango
125 ml (4 fl oz / ½ cup) melted
    coconut oil
1 vanilla pod (bean), scraped

To serve
fresh mango slices
raspberries
mint leaves
black sesame seeds

Add all the mousse ingredients to a high-speed blender and blitz until well incorporated.

The oil needs to completely emulsify with the mango, so make sure there are no white dots in the mix but it's just a beautiful orange colour.

Pour into individual glasses and let the mousse set in the fridge for 3 hours. Once set, top with fresh mango slices, raspberries, mint leaves and sprinkles of black sesame seeds for colour and crunch.

Tip

A great dessert to make way ahead of time!

BATCH COOKABLE

FREEZABLE

LASTS FOR +5 DAYS
IN THE FRIDGE

SPICY CARROT CAKE & TURMERIC FROSTING

I have had a love affair with carrot cake for as long as I can remember. This version contains lots of amazing spices and as many carrots as I could possibly fit in.

Serves 6

140 ml (5 fl oz / 1 cup) maple syrup
140 g (5 oz / 1 cup) Gluten-free Flour Mix (see page 146)
160 ml (5 fl oz / ⅔ cup) Almond Milk, shop-bought or home-made (see page 139)
½ teaspoon bicarbonate of soda (baking soda)
½ teaspoon baking powder
235 g (8 oz / 1½ cups) grated carrots
5 dried apricots, chopped
1 teaspoon ground cinnamon
½ teaspoon ground cloves
½ cardamom pod

For the turmeric frosting
160 g (5 oz / 1 cup) cashews, soaked for 2 hours, then drained
60 ml (2 fl oz / ¼ cup) maple syrup
60 ml (2 fl oz / ¼ cup) plant milk, shop-bought or home-made (see page 137–139)
1 teaspoon turmeric
1 vanilla pod (bean), scraped

To serve
berries and orange slices

Preheat the oven to 180°C (350°F/Gas 4). Line a 20cm (8 ins) round cake tin (pan) with greaseproof (wax) paper.

Put all the cake ingredients into a bowl and give it a really good mix. Transfer to the cake tin and bake in the oven for 40 minutes.

Turmeric frosting

In the meantime, add all the frosting ingredients to a blender and blitz until you have a lovely smooth consistency. Let the frosting cool in the fridge.

Once the cake is cooked, transfer to a wire rack until completely cool.

When cold, spoon the frosting over the top and decorate with blueberries or other berries and fruits of choice. Personally I love oranges as the flavour cuts through the sweetness and creaminess of the frosting. Also, they look pretty!

BATCH COOKABLE

FREEZABLE

LASTS FOR +5 DAYS
IN THE FRIDGE

BANOFFEE PIE

One of my favourite recipes in this book. This is a spoonful of heaven; sticky, sweet, spicy and indulgent. It's a plant-based take on a classic that I love dearly.

Makes 6 slices

For the base
185 g (6 oz / 1¾ cups) almond flour
80 g (3 oz / ½ cup) cashews
3 tablespoons coconut oil
pinch of salt

For the toffee filling
12 medjool dates, stoned (pitted)
  and soaked for 1 hour, plus
  3 tablespoons soaking liquid
1 tablespoon almond butter
1 vanilla pod (bean), scraped
pinch of salt

For the topping
1 batch of Vanilla Custard
  (see page 146)
3 bananas
3 tablespoons cacao powder
grated chocolate (optional)

Preheat the oven to 180°C (350°F/Gas 4).

In a blender, blitz the base ingredients until you get a lovely sticky consistency. Pour into a 20 cm (8 ins) cake tin (pan) or good-quality silicone mould and gently press down until you have a beautiful even base. It is nice to have a small edge just like you would with a classic pie. Make the edge by pushing your thumb on the inside of the casing and shaping with your other thumb from the top, working your way all around.

Cook in the oven for 10–15 minutes until golden brown. Once cooked, transfer to a wire rack to cool.

Toffee filling
While the base is cooking, make the toffee filling. Put all the ingredients into a blender and blitz until you have a beautiful sticky, toffee-like consistency. Set aside.

Once the base has cooled, pour the sticky toffee mixture into the pie casing and make sure you have an even layer.

Topping
Now do the same with the vanilla custard.

Slice the bananas and arrange on top of the custard. Finally, sift a layer of cacao powder on top and you are ready to go. If you are feeling fancy, grate some extra chocolate on top.

Tip
Cake base can be made raw; just pop in the freezer instead of the oven for an hour.

BATCH COOKABLE

FREEZABLE

+5
DAYS

LASTS FOR +5 DAYS
IN THE FRIDGE

BERRY CRUMBLE WITH COCONUT CREAM CUSTARD

Who doesn't love a good crumble? I do, because it makes me feel all warm and fuzzy on the inside. I like this cold and warm on a winter's evening. This is great as a breakfast dish, too!

Serves 6

600 g (1 lb 5 oz) mixed
  frozen berries
1 red or green apple, chopped
  into cubes
125 ml (4 fl oz / ½ cup) orange juice
  or juice from 2 fresh oranges
2 tablespoons coconut sugar
1 vanilla pod (bean), seeds scraped

For the crumble
35 g (1½ oz / ¼ cup) pistachios
35 g (1½ oz / ¼ cup) raw hazelnuts
90 g (3½ oz / 1 cup) oat bran
2 medjool dates, stoned (pitted)
35 ml (1½ fl oz / ⅛ cup) coconut oil
1 tablespoon maple syrup
pinch of salt

To serve
Vanilla Custard (see page 146)
dollop of Coconut Yoghurt,
  shop-bought or home-made
  (see page 142)

Preheat the oven to 170°C (340°F/Gas 3).

In a bowl combine the berries, apple, orange juice, coconut sugar and vanilla seeds and ladle into a large baking tray or 6 small ramekins.

Crumble

In a blender, blitz the crumble ingredients and pulse a few times until you have a chunky consistency – not too fine and not too chunky.

Spread the crumble over the berry mixture and cook in the oven for 45 minutes, possibly a bit longer if you like your topping crispy. Serve with custard or coconut yoghurt.

BLACK RICE PUDDING WITH MAPLE-GLAZED BANANAS

This lovely bowl of goodness comes from my time in Bali. A classic Balinese sweet that I put my own twist on. This also works a treat as a filling breakfast.

Serves 4

95 g (3½ oz / ½ cup) black rice
250 ml (8½ fl oz / 1 cup) water
250 ml (8½ fl oz / 1 cup) coconut milk
1 vanilla pod (bean)
3 tablespoons coconut sugar
2 bananas
1 teaspoon coconut oil
1 tablespoon maple syrup

To serve
dollop of Coconut Yoghurt, shop-bought or home-made (see page 142)
toasted coconut flakes
black sesame seeds
edible flowers (optional)

Start by boiling the rice in a medium pan with the water until all the liquid has completely evaporated. This should not take more than 20–30 minutes.

Add the coconut milk, vanilla pod and coconut sugar to the rice and let everything simmer for another 20 minutes until you have a beautiful, creamy rice pudding-like consistency.

While the pudding is simmering, slice the bananas horizontally and fry in a medium pan with the coconut oil. You want the bananas to turn slightly brown. Once cooked, finish them off with the maple syrup and black sesame seeds.

Once the rice pudding is done, ladle into bowls, top with the caramelised banana, a dollop of coconut yoghurt, sprinkles of toasted coconut flakes and edible flowers, if using.

Tip

This pudding is great made in advance and lasts for at least 3 days or more in the fridge.

BATCH COOKABLE

FREEZABLE

LASTS FOR +5 DAYS
IN THE FRIDGE

NUT-FREE

BANANA SPLIT

As a treat my mother used to take me to a very retro ice-cream parlour in Dar es Salaam, in Tanzania, where I grew up until the age of 11. They served this huge banana split with cream, chocolate sauce and a cherry on top. I am nostalgic like that and this dessert encapsulates all of those memories.

Serves 2–4

9 frozen bananas
3 tablespoons plant milk of your choice (shop bought or home made, see pages 137–139)
1 vanilla pod (bean), scraped
4 strawberries
2 tablespoons cacao powder

For the chocolate sauce
80 ml (2½ fl oz / ⅓ cup) coconut oil
4 tablespoons cacao powder
3 tablespoons maple syrup
pinch of salt
1 vanilla pod (bean), scraped

To serve
bananas, sliced horizontally
cherries
coconut flakes

Chocolate sauce   Start by making the chocolate sauce. Combine all the ingredients and gently heat through in a medium pan for about 5 minutes – make sure you don't overheat as this will separate the sauce. Once well combined, pour into a glass jar and set aside.

Ice cream   Now make the ice cream. You have three flavours here: vanilla, strawberries and chocolate. Separate the bananas into three clusters, one for each flavour.

In a blender, start with the vanilla flavour by adding the bananas, 1 tablespoon of plant milk and the vanilla. Once blended, store in a bowl and keep in the freezer until you need them. Do the same with the other two flavours, blitzing and blending them separately and store in 2 bowls in the freezer.

Get out the chocolate sauce and the three flavours of instant ice cream. Arrange the banana slices into pretty bowls or dishes out and top with one spoon of each ice cream and drizzles of chocolate sauce, finishing with a cherry and coconut flakes. Serve immediately.

Tip   If you have any leftover chocolate cookies, crumble them on the top for extra indulgence and crunch!

MENU

FRIDGE BASICS

Make these recipes and you have literally swapped the ordinary basics for plant-based versions. One of the hardest parts of adopting a fully plant-based diet, or once you have to make changes to how you eat after a discovering an allergy, is finding a delicious substitute for the everyday stuff: breads, milks, cheeses, etc.

So here are some great options – including some that will last in fridge for up to five days, so you can make them ahead and take the hassle out of catering for a new diet.

· Almond Milk (see page 139)
· Cashew Yoghurt (see page 140)
· Macadamia Ricotta (see page 144)
· Nut Parmesan (see page 145)
· Super Bread (see page 148)
· Big Batch Dressing (see page 152)

BRUNCHING IT

Weekends are for treats, so here are three options that will make the best brunch spread ever!

OPTION 1

GET AHEAD
The tea can be steeped the night before, as can the waffle and chickpea mixes, and refrigerated.

· Hearty Buckwheat Waffles with Strawberries (see page 24)
· Chickpea Omelette, Rocket, Avocado & Mango Salsa (see page 34)
· Warming Coconut Chai Tea (see page 41)

OPTION 2

GET AHEAD
The French toast has to be made to order, but make the batter the day before and refrigerating. Make the bread in advance.

· Almond Butter & Smashed Raspberry Stuffed French Toast (see page 28)
· Hot Spicy Chocolate with Vanilla (see page 37)
· Avocado on Toast the Bettina's Kitchen Way (see page 47)

OPTION 3

GET AHEAD
The banana pancake mix can be made a day ahead, as can the focaccia.

· Banana Pancakes with Home-made Nut-ella (see page 26)
· Baked Shakshuka with Butter Beans, Topped with Avocado (see page 64)
· Rosemary & Garlic Focaccia (to dip into the shakshuka) (see page 122)

PLANS

BREAKFAST ON THE GO!

Midweek easy recipes that are perfect for eating on the go and great for the morning commute. These are the quickest breakfast recipes out of the lot and can be prepared ahead in batches.

OPTION 1

GET AHEAD
All of these recipes can be prepared the day before and put in the fridge overnight.

· Peanut Butter Overnight Oats & Home-made Granola Crunch (see page 22)
· Pistachio Milk Chia Pudding in a Jar (see page 31)
· One-cup Sticky Banana Bread (see page 32)
· Salted Caramel Smoothie (see page 39)

For the slow and slightly chilly midweek mornings, when you wake up 30 minutes early and you have some extra time to get yourself started with a warm, hearty breakfast.

OPTION 2

GET AHEAD
These recipes can be prepared the day before and reheated with a splash of plant milk the next morning.

• Bright Healing Turmeric Porridge & Warm Berries (see page 19)
• Slow-cooked Oats & Buckwheat Porridge with Caramelised Apple (see page 20)
• Warming Coconut Chai Tea (see page 24)

LUNCH IN A BOX

Great takeaway recipes for work lunch boxes or picnics. There is some prepping involved for these recipes because there is more than one element to each of them, but once you have put the hard work in you will have lunch ready for a few days.

GET AHEAD
If you can, give yourself a slow day to prep all of these recipes then put them together on the day you need them.

· Spicy Thai Noodles, Creamy Peanut Dressing (see page 50)
· My Favourite Quinoa Bowl, Veggies, Beans & Basil Mayo (see page 54)
· Mexican Bowl – Black Beans, Guacamole and Oven-roasted Sweet Potatoes (see page 55)
· Garlic & Onion-fried Rice, Fresh Sambal, Mashed Avocado & Red Onion (see page 58)
· Epic Veggie Sandwich (see page 66)
· Bibimbap – Korean Rice Bowl with All the Sides (see page 86)

DINNER PARTIES

SUMMER PARTY

OPTION 1
GET AHEAD
Prep the nut cheese the day before, then the rest of the preparations can be done in the morning ready to assemble later.

· Loaded Tacos Walnut Mince & Apple Slaw (see page 88)
· Griddled Chilli Pineapple, Mixed greens & Marie Rose (see page 103)
· Tomato, Spicy Rocket, Watermelon & Compressed Feta Salad (see page 102)

OPTION 2
GET AHEAD
This can all be prepared the day before, so all you need to do on the day of your party is put it together and serve it beautifully.

· Truffled Cashew Cheese and Caramelised Pears with Seeded Crackers (see page 96)
· Wicked Potato Salad with Dill (see page 117)
· Nan's Sweet & Sour Pickles (see page 125)
· Smoky Sumac Green Beans (see page 126)
· The Best Non-meatballz Ever (see page 154)
· Strawberry & Cream Cake (see page 164)

SUNDAY 'ROAST' KIND OF THING

These are great combinations that go really well together as family/friend feasts. The best dinners are those where you can share the fun by picking and eating different flavours that are all meshed into one meal.

OPTION 1
GET AHEAD
All of the food items can be cooked the day before and reheated. Curry always tastes better a day or two after making, so that the flavours really infuse the dish. I would cook the steamed rice and bread fresh.

Starter
Creamy Coconut Red Lentil Dal (see page 118) with Chickpea Flatbread & Marinated Crunchy Chickpeas (see page 130)

Main
Curry with All the Sides: Minty Raita & Crunchy Coconut Topper (see page 110)

Dessert
The Easiest Mango Vanilla Mousse (see page 172)

OPTION 2
GET AHEAD
You can get ahead the day before by chopping up all your vegetables ready to go. The chocolate mousse is also better prepped the day before. On the day of your event, cook the starters and mains just before serving.

Starter
Garden Vegetable Soup with Fresh Herbs (see page 56)

Main
Multi-vegetable Paella & Avo Aioli (see page 106)

Dessert
Easy Peasy Chocolate Mousse (see page 172)

OPTION 3

GET AHEAD
The sweet potato cakes can be prepped the day before and just cooked on the day along with the cashew yoghurt. The meatballz can be assembled the day before, refrigerated overnight and cooked on the day. Berry crumble can be put together the day before, ready to go into the oven along with a freshly made custard that takes no time.

Starter
Sweet Potato Cakes
with Dill & Cashew Yoghurt (see page 81)

Main
Swedish Non-meatballz, Carrot Mash,
Gravy & Nan's Pickles (see page 100)

Dessert
Berry Crumble with Coconut Cream Custard
(see page 176)

OPTION 4

GET AHEAD
The crust of the pizza can be pre-made and kept in the fridge until ready to use. The vegetables can be prepared the day before ready to go into the oven and cooked fresh. Sticky toffee pudding is a great dessert to make the day before. Gently reheat on the day.

Starter
Hazelnut Crust Pizza & Peppery Rocket
(see page 76)

Main
Mario's Italian Stuffed Veggies (see page 82),
Polenta with Oven-roasted Tomatoes & Sweet,
Sticky Garlic (see page 78),
Rosemary & Garlic Focaccia (see page 122)

Dessert
Sticky Toffee Pudding with Sticky Toffee Sauce
(see page 168)

MOVIE NIGHT!

Easy, quick and super-comforting meals. Forget the takeaway and give these a go! Some are snack alternatives to your usual crisps and popcorn, and other are options for meals that you might usually prepare for a night in.

- One-pot Green Curry in a Hurry (see page 48)
- Spicy Thai Noodles with Creamy Peanut Dressing (see page 50)
- Pasta Pesto & Nut Parmesan (see page 53)
- Epic Veggie Sandwich (see page 66)
- Juicy Tomato Spaghetti & Non-meatballz (see page 74)
- Hazelnut Crust Pizza & Peppery Rocket (see page 76)
- Maple-glazed Sesame Kale Crisps (see page 123)
- Hazelnut Bites (see page 160)
- Chocolate Chip Cookies (see page 162)
- Banana Split (see page 180)

WINTER WARMERS

Yummy, soothing recipes that will satisfy you on a cold winter evening. These recipes are here because they warm your heart from the inside out. If you have had a tough day and need to be comforted, these are great suggestions. They vary in the time it takes to cook them – some can even be batch-cooked and eaten over more than one day. One thing is for sure, though, they will make you feel good.

- Korean Pancake, Sliced Roots & Chilli Sweet & Sour Tamari (see page 60)
- My Mother's Comforting Bean Soup (see page 63)
- Baked Shakshuka with Butter Beans, Topped with Avocado (see page 64)
- Man-flu Soup, Noodles, Ginger, Garlic, Onions & Lots of Spice (see page 73)
- Polenta with Oven-roasted Tomatoes & Sweet, Sticky Garlic (see page 78)

Thank Yous

Thank you to everyone who has supported me on this crazy journey of life. My family and friends. All the people I have gotten to know and worked with over the years. A huge thank you to Hardie Grant for making this a reality, to Kate Pollard for believing in me as well as my agent Becky Thomas, and the amazing team behind this book – Nassima Rothacker, Evi O, Wei Tang and Jess Dennison. Thank you also to Gaya Ceramics for lending me some beautiful ceramics for the shoot. Last but not least, I would like to thank every single person who's followed and supported me on social media – regardless of what people say, the support and friendships I have made are the real deal!

Humbled and eternally grateful.

About Bettina

Bettina Campolucci Bordi is a freelance chef and food blogger who specialises in vegan and gluten-free cuisine. Cooking has been a constant in Bettina's life, following her through her teens and into adulthood. She's run workshops, advised clients on food intolerances and allergies, consulted on recipes, launched pop-ups, hosted retreats around the world, and built a large, loyal Instagram following. This is her first book.

bettinaskitchen.com   @bettinas_kitchen

INDEX

Published in 2018 by Hardie Grant Books,
an imprint of Hardie Grant Publishing

Hardie Grant Books (London)
5th & 6th Floors
52–54 Southwark Street
London SE1 1UN

Hardie Grant Books (Melbourne)
Building 1, 658 Church Street
Richmond, Victoria 3121

hardiegrantbooks.com

British Library Cataloguing-in-Publication Data.
A catalogue record for this book is available from the British Library.

Happy Food by Bettina Bordi Campolucci
ISBN: 978-1-78488-157-3

Publisher: Kate Pollard
Publishing Assistant: Eila Purvis
Art Direction: Evi O. / Evi O. Studio
Illustrations: Jo Wright / Evi O. Studio
Photographer: Nassima Rothacker
Photography Assistant: Maria Aversa
Food Assistant: Jess Dennison
Editor: Helena Caldon
Proofreader: Kay Delves
Indexer: Cathy Heath

Colour Reproduction by p2d
Printed and bound in China by 1010